VINTAGE LORRY

ALBUM

COMPILED & EDITED by NICK BALDWIN

PUBLISHED BY
MARSHALL HARRIS & BALDWIN LTD
17 AIR STREET LONDON W1

Our efforts to clear up the complexities of Pierce-Arrow radiators were not completely successful, so here is another one from the Union Cartage fleet showing the familiar radiator but ungilled first line of tubes.

Since telling the W&G story in *LORRY ANNUAL NO 1* we have found this interesting view of a motor caravan built on an Austin chassis in 1909 by Arthur du Cros. The du Cros family were, of course, major Austin shareholders and we show many of Austin's later lorries in this *ALBUM*.

FOREWORD

SINCE the first *LORRY ALBUM* (or *ANNUAL* as we then called it) we have had mountains of mail. Rather than print all the interesting comments in full and thus take up too much valuable space, we thought that a quick run-through of key parts of them might suffice, but can assure correspondents that we have noted all the wider issues and incorporated many of them in this volume. Several people commented on the difficulty of working out which caption went with which photo in the Transworld Trucks feature. Our apologies - we kept getting extra pictures and cramming them in until it all became a bit of a hotch-potch - but nevertheless an interesting one, as several people confirmed. Malcolm Keeley said that a contents page or index would be vital when several albums were side by side on his shelves, and we agree, and have included a comprehensive index for both Nos 1 and 2 in this edition. For No 1 to be effective, you have to number your own pages, starting with 1 as the title page and 2 as 'Introducing Ourselves'.

There was a very mixed reaction to the inclusion of post-war articles and Douglas, being an off-beat subject, came in for particular criticism on this score. Frankly, we were a little disappointed with this reaction as we wanted to give as broad a spread of subjects as possible. In general, we suspect that it was older readers who wanted us to stick to vintage in its most precise definition, and unfortunately not enough younger readers told us what they thought (unless Nick Georgano and Bart Vanderveen count as youngsters, in which case they both liked the Douglas article!). Anyway, because it is both post-war and a minority subject, we have not included the Vickers-AWD story in this issue.

Graham Dix wants to see more on heavy haulage and construction industry vehicles. We like the idea and are thinking of separate volumes on the former subject and perhaps a one-off book on off-road vehicles in general. Norman Garner wants some really detailed articles or books on Dennis and Thornycroft and we certainly plan to follow up our forthcoming book on AEC with one on Dennis.

Now to some specific points about the articles in No 1. Chris Taylor mentions that Rutland was another user of the original Motor Panels cab, and we are fairly sure that Vulcan also used

it on some tractive units for BRS - does anyone have photos of either type?

In the Transworld Trucks feature, Bart Vanderveen is very suspicious of the 4x4 Mercedes on page 26 and says that, whilst its cab and radiator are right, the rest has a 'junkyard special' look about it. The Chevrolet underneath may be just that or a Ford F60L with Chevrolet grille and front shell. He puts the c1930 Chevrolet in Majorca at 1933 and the Buick 8 at 1936. The Dodge on p27 is a D15 4x2 15 cwt of 1941 with non-standard rear wheel arrangement and the disguised Mercedes under it has GMC not Chevrolet sheet metal. Resulting from the Trucks or Tracks article, David Nicholas tells us that the Morris Roadless Tractor was a civilian spin-off from the 8 Martell tanketts that Morris had made for the War Office and that both suffered from chronic steering difficulties because the wheels lost contact with the ground when the throttle was eased off! The Morris on page 20 was apparently known as a Tractor No 3 and was built for gun pulling, having been tested by the MWEE in 1928. David Nicholas has also seen photographs of this vehicle with large, but otherwise conventional, rear wheels. He also has details of a Vulcan-FWD half track (MWEE 62) in 1926 which is not the one shown, and he would like to know what it looked like. In the Sheppee article the son of the Mr Jowitt mentioned has written to point out that the original firm's initials were PTL not PLT and that his father deserves credit for much of Sheppee's advanced development.

The extraordinary 8x8 vehicle in 'Trains off Tracks' (p49) has caused several people to scratch their heads and we agree that the one shown is the 1932 Leyland. From fresh pictures that we have now seen, it would seem that the 1933 AEC differed in steering on only the two outer axles. Of course, it had a diesel in place of the Leyland's petrol engine, though this does not show up in any of the photos. Perhaps the easiest distinguishing feature is that the AEC has large hub reduction bulges on each wheel, the axles presumably being ex-FWD/Hardy.

The Internationals in *Seen and Heard* were seen at Iola, not Hershey, and Bart says that the 4x4 is an M-3H-4 1½ tonner used almost exclusively by the US Navy. This type of 150 inch wheelbase model was equipped during the war for fire fighting by American La France, whilst the slightly more common (1080 against 210) M-3L-4 of 139 inch wheelbase had American Bean equipment). He is not certain whether the one shown was originally built as a fire truck, however.

On the subject of the W&G article, Chris Taylor points out that the firm must have anticipated building more vehicles than they actually did because they often took 3-4 years to use up some of their orders for Dorman engines. The bus on page 81 was new in July 1924 and appears to have been round the trade in South Wales before going to a Barry operator in 1927 'with flats on its tyres from standing'. It was soon replaced by a Gilford and then went to Hever of Dartford, where the photograph was probably taken.

In *Seen & Heard* on page 45 of *LORRY ANNUAL NO 1*, we tried to clear up the variations on the Pierce-Arrow radiators shown in our last issue of *OLD MOTOR* (11:6 - *Tea and Wads*) and seem to have got even more mixed up. What John Bland actually said was that the Riker and its forerunner, the Locomobile, used wider apart fins on their header tank castings than Pierce-Arrow did and an example of the Riker type is shown on p323 of *OM* 11:4 between Hallford and Thornycroft radiators. The Pierce-Arrow radiator normally had gilled tubes, not the smooth ones shown on page 437 of 11:6, but through a magnifying glass we can see that only the front tubes are like this, probably having had the gills removed after they had become bent and clogged. We show another gill-less Pierce-Arrow from the same Union Cartage fleet, by courtesy of Jack Sparshatt. Arthur Cox worked for Union Cartage at the time and wrote to say that he remembers the puncture troubles they suffered when the Pierce-Arrows were switched to Avon pneumatics about 1929. The Pierce-Arrows were ex-WD and supplied by Lawson Piggott Motors, King's Street, Hammersmith. The Bernas were four cylinder petrol and arrived in about 1930 and were followed by a few with 6 cylinder Deutz-licence engines. The Leyland Bulls, of which there were three, were six cylinder petrol engined and new in 1932. The matchboard van bodies were made by Union Cartage in their Sancroft Street, Kennington, body shop. Union Cartage livery was dark green with black wings, red wheels and white lettering.

Finally, Martin Wallast has written to say his book on the Dutch industry reviewed on p96 cost 47.50 *Guilders* not pounds! Apologies.

We look forward to hearing your comments on No 2 and to having any corrections and amplifications that you can point out so that the Albums can build up into a full and authoritative reference work.

CONFESSIONS OF A PAVEMENT BASHER

**One of the best known motoring historians, G N GEORGANO,
became a keen convert to lorries when he saw what was still in use
on the Continent in the fifties. Here he shows a random selection
of the rare and appealing vehicles that he has photographed
over the years.**

IT all started during my first foreign
holiday, a ten-day family jaunt to
Brittany in July 1950. Although
interested in vehicles, and particularly
commercials, since early childhood, it
had never occurred to me to take

photographs of them, but suddenly
faced with a fascinating variety of
strange machines (in those pre-
Common Market days practically
everything on French roads was
strange to English eyes), and with a

brand new Baby Brownie camera in
my hands, what could be more natural
than to take my own photos to add to
my collection of cuttings from *The
Commercial Motor, Modern Transport* and *Bus & Coach*? Film was still

One of the features of Spanish traffic in the early 1960s was the considerable number of ZIS-5 lorries of Russian origin which had been supplied to the Republican forces during the Civil War. Most of them had their petrol engines replaced by Perkins diesels. The letters ZIS look very like 3HC in the Russian alphabet, and Spaniards nicknamed them *Tres Hermanos Communistas* [Three Communist Brothers].

in short supply (so was pocket money) and that first year I took only eight photos; the following year I returned to Brittany and took 24; since then I have quite lost count, but my total of cars and commercial vehicles, taken in fourteen countries, must run to 10,000 or more.

The delight of France in the early 1950s, and Spain ten years later, was the number of elderly vehicles still at work. Obviously one can no longer expect to find vintage specimens in the 1980s, and even 1950s trucks seem much thinner on the ground than twenty-year-olds were when I began my 'pavement bashing', but there is still such a variety of commercial vehicles to be found that it does not matter if they are not particularly old. One of the delights of the hobby is that, provided one has reasonable weather and a camera loaded with film, one is never bored in any city on earth. It is a fine way of getting to know a place and seeing areas never dreamt of by the conventional tourist -- in this way I have felt almost a native of Madrid, Zurich, Geneva, Vienna, Philadelphia and New York, and, to a lesser extent, of Warsaw, Leningrad and Moscow.

Troubles and awkward incidents have been astonishingly few; only twice have I been actually forbidden to take a photo. The first occasion was of a police car in Helsinki and the second a derelict aerodynamic Adler which was inside the compound of the local prison in the Southern Spanish town of Murcia. Drivers are understandably suspicious of one's motives -- as a burly Negro in Philadelphia said, 'We t'ought you was working for de bosses' but once one explains that one is just a truck nut, a friendly 'help yourself' nearly always results. Here is just a small selection from the photographs I have taken over the last 30 years -- I hope you will find them of interest.

The first photo I ever took was of this mid-1920s Renault pick-up truck, possibly converted from a private car, outside the Café du Port, St Jacut de la Mer, Brittany, July 1950.

French fairgrounds, like their British counterparts, were wonderful repositories of elderly vehicles. This solid tyred Berliet CB must date from the early 1920s, and was taken at St Jacut de la Mer in July 1951.

Perl was quite a well-known Austrian make of light and medium sized lorries and buses [including electrics] in the inter-war period. This is a 30 cwt D4 model of about 1932, snapped at Seefeld, Austrian Tyrol, in September 1958. Note the sacking to protect the tyres from the heat of the sun.

Another attractive Austrian lorry was this small Graf & Stift, taken in Vienna in 1959.

By comparison, here is a ZIS-5 on its home ground, taken in Leningrad in 1962. The squared-off mudguards give it a military air, though such vehicles were supplied for civilian work as well. It is difficult to date, as lorries of this type were made from 1934 to 1944. They were by no means uncommon in Russia in 1962; most were open trucks like this one, but I saw one delightful box van with two-wheeled van trailer, the whole ensemble painted in a dual colour scheme of blue and cream.

The original appearance of the old lorries in Spain was often spoilt by modernised cabs, as on this Italian SPA, the bonnet of which dates it as early 1930s. Taken in Madrid, April 1962.

In no European country did old commercials survive for so long as in Spain. This line-up, by no means untypical, was seen in Seville as late as 1965. On the left are two Dodge 3 tonners [with non-standard cabs], and next to them a Studebaker, all *circa* 1932.

The small Croydon firm of Motor Traction Limited exported many of their vehicles to Spain, and this Rutland M4 3 tonner was seen in Seville in April 1965.

Back to England for this one, an ex-military Thornycroft Nubian 4x4, taken at Whitecroft in the Forest of Dean in April 1964. The Nubian was in the same class as the Bedford QL, but was nothing like as common.

Another ex-military vehicle, a 4x4 Crossley Q type, originally used by the RAF for recovery work, and still employed for road resurfacing in South Kensington in 1968.

Latil is associated in British eyes with the Traulier 4x4 tractors assembled by Shelvoke & Drewry in the 1930s, but the Suresnes firm made many other types, including this *circa* 1938 streamlined furniture van, seen in Madrid in 1965.

*C*1938 Alfa Romeo Model T500, one of three at work in the docks at Cadiz in 1965.

A General Motors product in Switzerland, this 1938 Bedford 2 tonner was seen in Spiez in 1968. It was one of three delivered to Radio Steiner of Berne, who used them as door-to-door service vans for radio sets, and occasionally for outside broadcast work as they were fitted with transmitters. In its 1968 guise it was a mobile greengrocer's shop. Despite its flat front it is not a forward control vehicle, for the driver sits behind the engine, and that enormous expanse of glass surrounds a conventional bonnet.

Normal control electric vans have always been pretty rare beasts, though Morrison-Electricar made a few in the 1930s. This is a Swiss built SIG EL300 made in 1943, and still used by a dairy at Versoix on the shores of Lake Geneva in 1967.

A Vauxhall variant never seen in Britain was this light van based on the LIX series Wyvern of 1948/51. They were widely used by the Swiss Post Office. Zurich, September 1963.

French vintage vehicles were not particularly common in Spain when I was there, apart from small Renaults and Citroëns. This is, therefore, quite a rarity, a c1926 De Dion Bouton. There was no equivalent of the MoT test in Spain in 1965, which was fortunate as the jagged nearside wing and bald offside front tyre would hardly have impressed the testers.

Another unusual American producer of light vehicles, though well known for its larger chain drive, wooden flitched chassis trucks, was Sterling, who built this DB-7 1¼ tonner in 1930. It was photographed in Madrid in 1962.

A German heavy, looking rather more suited to thundering down Autobahns than delivering coal in Madrid, was this c1936 Büssing.

A considerably modified Liberty-Willeme heavy wrecker from the 1930s. These were built by the French company, originally closely based on the American World War One Liberty trucks. The operators of this one, Transportes El Checa of Madrid, had a number of odd vehicles, apparently assembled from ex-World War Two American army trucks.

From the 1920s to the 1950s there was quite a vogue in Germany and Switzerland for the road tractor pulling a drawbar trailer. The smaller of these were simply agricultural tractors with road equipment. This is a late example, a Swiss made Hurlimann diesel, Lucerne 1963.

A larger road tractor, also Swiss, was this *c*1930 Berna, taken in Lucerne in September 1963. Unlike the Hurlimann [a firm which still makes agricultural tractors], the Berna design is plainly lorry-based.

One of the toughest commercial vehicle makes, to judge from the elderly examples still around, was the Swiss Saurer. Here is one seen in Malaga in 1964 dating from about 1930, which may have been re-engined by Barreiros.

The Swiss Army cherished their vehicles and this 1937 Berna 1½ tonner was still in use during autumn manoeuvres in 1966.

Although this White Diesel is not particularly rare or old, I cannot resist including the photo as I have always been puzzled as to how the driver got into this predicament. Was he trying to make a U turn, or did he swerve to avoid a dog? Whatever the cause, it looks as if extricating him would be a pretty awkward task. Were the helpers encouraged by the posters in the background saying that 'Everything goes better with Coca-Cola'? Madrid, April 1966.

50 YEARS OF ROAD HAULAGE IN WALES

We are always delighted to publish the recollections of transport operators of long ago, particularly when they have had as long a career as TECWYN ROBERTS, and have run so many interesting vehicles spanning the eras of steam, petrol and diesel.

LIKE so many early haulage contractors, W H Roberts started his business immediately after the Great War using war surplus vehicles, in his case Sentinels and FWDs. Originally trading as Roberts and Rice Jones (the borough surveyor at Ruthin) Building & Haulage Contractors, the partnership lasted until 1924 when W H

Roberts' son, Tecwyn, joined his father. Tecwyn Roberts remembers their first FWD well: 'It was a three tonner with all wheel drive. It had a 4 cylinder Wisconsin 36hp engine of low compression, in two blocks of two cylinders. The cylinder head could not be removed, but had valve caps in order to get at the inlet and exhaust

W H Roberts was encouraged to buy a Sentinel steamer in 1920 by the good performance of Ellis' 1912 four tonner which delivered mineral water from his home town.

valves. As with most, if not all, motor vehicles of the period, there was no self-starter, the engine having to be swung over with a starting handle. One of advantage of this was that one

The original partnership ran an ex-War Office FWD like this. It had very flexible suspension which led to various minor difficulties and one major one - it fell over when unequally loaded.

The Roberts' bought some 4 ton Sentinels in 1928 and then this late twenties Super in 1930, shown here loading coal at Ruthin station. The driver and mate are William Jones and Ernest Thomas.

The Super Sentinel again, this time collecting a load of tarmac from the local lime quarry.

could check the compression according to the resistance. The valves, being rather soft, would distort and then dig holes in the seating!

'The maximum speed was about 12 to 15 mph, whilst petrol consumption was about 4 miles per gallon at 1/3d (6½p) per gallon. The drive was through a 3 speed gearbox more or less in the centre of the chassis, with a central differential in unit with it underneath. From this, the drive was via propeller shafts to the front and rear axle. This centre diff could be locked if required on soft ground, otherwise all the drive could pass to one individual wheel.

'On getting back on to hard ground one had to be careful to disconnect this lock, otherwise there would be a strain on the transmission when turning bends or attempting to turn around, as the front wheels, when locked over, would be trying to turn a larger radius than those on the rear axle. These FWD vehicles were far better on rough or hilly ground than single driving axle vehicles, but traction was still rather limited, because of their solid tyres.

'The front springs were fixed at their forward ends, whilst the rear ends rested in brackets under the chassis in which they were free to slide back and forth according to the amount of weight on the chassis. The rear springs were fixed at their forward end to a bracket and spring pin. Their rear end was coupled to the end of a transverse spring hanging upside down under and across the chassis, with two coupled links fixed to the spring ends by shackles.

'This made for easy riding, but unless the load was reasonably balanced, the body could weigh down very much on one side. In fact, I remember one occasion when one half of the load had been unloaded, lengthwise, and on going to turn around the vehicle fell over on its side! The cab, being ex-Army, was a high back board behind the driver, with a canvas roof reaching over the front of the vehicle, open forward and to the sides - with no other protection! The driver and his mate sat above the engine, suitably protected from the heat, of course!

Perhaps one of the water refill points that the Roberts' used when collecting animal feeds from Lancashire. This one is preserved by Merseyside County Museums.

L.C.W.W.

MOTOR WAGON SUPPLY

The shape of things to come - the British assembled 1930 Chevrolet 1½ tonner was found to be ideal for the narrow lanes and steep hills around Ruthin.

'The handbrake was two lined steel bands tightening on the outside of two drums, and was very poor and of no use on hills. The footbrake was a 4 inch wide band contracting on a 10 inch wheel immediately behind the gearbox, driven by a plate or flange from the centre of which a shaft protruded into the gearbox. This plate was bolted on by 8 or 10 coarse thread bolts, which sometimes loosened off, so that, if one did not realise in time, could work right off! Result - no footbrake. I have recollections of this happening on a long hill down towards Ruthin. My father steered, whilst I pulled as hard as I could on the handbrake. However, I could not slow it down, so all he could do was to drive the vehicle obliquely against a wall, which fortunately stopped it before any serious damage could occur and before reaching a U-bend!

'Another habit the FWD had was for the driving shafts, being soft, to twist and break, which of course left one without a footbrake. Although this happened on two or three occasions, fortunately no harm resulted, as there was a soft bank available in each case. After an axle shaft had broken, one could drive away by locking the centre differential and driving on the front or rear axle according to which one was unbroken.

'The throttle worked by a lever sticking up through the footplate, and operated by pushing it sideways from right to left with the right foot. This could become tiring for the foot, especially if held open for a long period against a strong spring. Relief could be had, however, by setting a hand lever to the required position, according to throttle requirements'.

As well as the FWD, W H Roberts and Son soon bought a Ford TT for lighter duties:

'It had the same engine as the Model T Ford car, rated at 25 hp on the old system. This engine was fitted into a chassis with a worm drive rear axle instead of the crown wheel and bevel pinion of the car, which gave it a lower axle ratio. Incidentally, in the car axle the crown wheel could be fitted either way so that one was driving backwards in forward gear!

'The gears, as on the car, were by planet and star wheels for low and reverse gear, obtained by pressing a

R.ROBERTS & SON, HAULAGE CONTRACTORS. RUTHIN.

UN 4499

Having been forced to abandon their steamer, W H Roberts & Son kept their allegiance to Sentinel and bought one of their new Austin 20 engined Garners, whose production had just been moved from Birmingham to the Sentinel factory at Shrewsbury [now the home of Rolls-Royce diesel engines and rail locos].

Another view of the 1935 Sentinel Garner with Emlyn Williams, its driver, on the left and the author of this article, Tecwyn Roberts.

The Roberts fleet in 1935 with, from left to right, a 1933 Morris-Commercial C Type, 1933 and 1932 Bedford two tonners with third axle conversions, a 1935 Bedford 1½ ton tipper, the Sentinel Garner 5-6 tonner, the Chevrolet 1½ tonner, a 1930 Guy 3 ton tipper and a 1934 Bedford 2-3 ton tipper.

pedal to brake the outer planet wheel. When this wheel was stopped, the Ford was fully in forward low or reverse gear. There were only two speeds and high gear was obtained by engaging a clutch, giving a direct drive from engine to propeller shaft. The hand-brake lever was used to hold this clutch out of engagement for free engine, and also to engage low and reverse gear, for which the handbrake lever was only partly drawn on. The handbrake lever operated expanding shoes in a drum on the rear axle, but was not particularly efficient. The footbrake operated on a drum similar to the gear planet wheels and was quite good.

'Electric current for ignition and lighting was supplied by a flywheel magneto or dynamo. For ignition, the current went to trembler coils on the dashboard and then on via a commutator (distributor) to the plugs. These commutators wore out very quickly, whilst if main bearings were worn laterally the moving flywheel and stationary backplate would move apart and would then not provide sufficient current for a hand start (there was no self-starter). The lighting was by direct current to the

Driver Dick Smith with 5/6 tons aboard a 1933 Bedford 2 ton chassis converted to three axles by Muir-Hill. It performed surprisingly well but with only one driven axle it often got stuck when delivering to farms.

Cheap, simple, strong and powerful Bedfords made an enormous impact on road haulage in the thirties. This is Roberts' 1934 two ton, three way tipper with its driver Emlyn Williams before he was promoted to the Garner. The only really bad feature of the early Bedfords were their poor brakes.

One of the early British 4-5 ton Dodges of 1935 with a coachbuilt cab [they were often supplied as chassis/scuttles]. The driver is Ted Atkinson and the man standing is the firm's clerk, Cecil Roberts. The Dodge was thirsty but an excellent hillclimber thanks to a five speed gearbox.

two headlamps in series, so that the strength of the lighting was controlled by the speed of the engine. Thus travelling at low engine speed meant a very poor light, whilst over-revving or travelling practically all-out - about 20 or so miles per hour - meant that a bulb might blow, leaving one entirely without a light! The throttle and ignition advance were worked by two levers, one on either side of the steering wheel.

'This vehicle became very popular with small contractors of all kinds, and also very many were used as delivery vans. The TT was the forerunner of the other successful 1 ton carrying capacity vehicles in the twenties, like the Morris-Commercial, Dodge and Chevrolet'.

In 1920 W H Roberts and his first partner bought another heavy vehicle and one that was very different from the FWD. It was Sentinel five ton tipper which was used with a trailer to collect alum from Runcorn and Birkenhead water works near Corwen, North Wales. Tecwyn Roberts recalls:

'This was fairly straightforward work, except that the Sentinel could only cross the Dee at Queensferry whilst empty, but had to come back via Chester loaded owing to the weight limit placed on the old Queensferry bridge (now demolished). Getting to the waterworks was rather tough, but the trailer could be parked, and the load delivered later. One fault with all the early Sentinels - up to the DG - was that with the direct drive from the crankshaft to the rear axle, the engine could stop with the valves in such a position that it could not restart, especially in soft ground. This is where a 2 or 3-speed vehicle had a sufficiently low gear, together with play in the gears, to restart. The engine was big and powerful, of course, and it was surprising where it could go, even if sometimes we had to move the control

lever backwards and forwards to rock it out of potholes.

'There was also a 4 tonner produced by Sentinel, all of the earlier ones (pre-1914) running on steel wheels with crossbars, similar to agricultural vehicles. These were slightly lighter vehicles, running on a higher gear. I cannot remember any of these as tippers, as this made them much heavier, reducing the payload, and also breaking the law. We acquired a Super Sentinel in 1930 - a tipper - which weighed, with water and fuel, 7 tons 5 cwt, against a maximum gross vehicle weight of 12 tons, allowing only 4 ton 15 cwt for the payload! In the early years - 1920s - not a great deal of notice was taken of this, but later the police became very keen. We got out of this generally by using a trailer, but at times it was hardly worth using a trailer for the weight of load required. This later Sentinel had

A little 30 cwt three way Bedford tipper new to W H Roberts and Son in 1938.

a high-sided body and if the police were short of a case, they would pull the vehicle in and, more often than not, it was overloaded, so they were able to convict. However, at one period the sides had been taken off, and the vehicle went in and out of Liverpool without any bother. Then came the time when the sides were replaced and immediately the police pounced, saying, 'Where have you been, we haven't seen you for a long time''.

'Another point with the tipper especially was that there was so much weight at the front, what with the boiler, up to ½ ton of fuel and the water tank, that when there was no load the vehicle could easily skid, having very little weight on the rear axle and that on solid tyres.

'The brakes also operated on the rear wheels only, a band contracting on a drum being the handbrake or parking brake. The normal and emergency brake, being the same one, was very powerful. The valves were moved to reverse position when the rear wheels could be locked. The braking effect could be controlled by a foot-controlled lever releasing the pressure every so often.

'Another necessity for steam

wagons, naturally, was to pick up water and this had to be done every 10 miles or so. This meant that there were picking-up points every so often, whilst in Birkenhead and Liverpool water could be drawn up at standpipes the keys for which could be borrowed from the local councils for a charge. This could be a difficulty today, as what with road widening, additional traffic and other matters, there are hardly any picking-up places for 'water.

'The Sentinel differed from the Fodens and other makes in that the driver actually drove and steered the vehicle with his mate stoking up the boiler to keep a head of steam, as against the driver on these other vehicles driving the engine and fuelling the boiler whilst the mate steered.

'I remember one of these other vehicles in the 1920s, a Tasker Little Giant, which was carrying bricks to a fairly local agricultural college. On entering the town, the vehicle had to turn left to deliver its load. On this particular day the steerer began to turn left as he approached the cross-roads. The vehicle did not slow down sufficiently for it to get round and it ran into the front of an empty corner shop, with the front wheels over-hanging the cellar! Apparently the driver had omitted to tell the steerer

that he intended to deliver the load the following day and had, therefore, not slowed down as usual to negotiate the corner!

'Of course, roads 60 or more years ago were not to be compared with today's, and whilst crossing the mountain from Ffestiniog to Pentre-foelas (North Wales), our Sentinel actually sank in the middle of the road. Another similar incident occurred in Ruthin, in Well Street, where a huge hole appeared under the vehicle and it turned out that water had washed away the foundations of the road! One frosty day a vehicle was going very gingerly on ice when it was caught up by an Austin Seven car. The car could not pass for some reason, so the driver braked and started skidding. The vehicle, being a tipper, had nothing much under the tail, which was fortunate for the car driver as his car skidded to a stop right under the tail-end of the steamer and was none the worse.

'One day, one of our vehicles was coming down a long hill 3 or 4 miles out of town where there was a steep drop away from the road on the left side. The driver's mate drew the driver's attention to what appeared to be a piece of the solid tyre flicking around. The driver stopped the vehicle and got down to have a look at the wheel. Apparently, the wheel had

A five ton Austin which dated from 1953 and had a Perkins P6 diesel. In general the short wheelbase vehicles were used on roadworks and the longer ones for local deliveries and collecting animal feed from mills in Lancashire and elsewhere.

stopped on the split piece of rubber so he asked his mate to reverse the vehicle. Unfortunately, the steam lever came off in the mate's hand and fell to the floor (it had a square hole fitting onto the squared end of the throttle lever). To prevent the vehicle continuing in reverse, he thrust the lever to forward and bent down to pick up the lever. When he raised his head, the vehicle was about to run off the road and all he could do was to jump off just before the vehicle finally went through the hedge. Luckily, there were a number of trees below the road just there, which eventually stopped it. To get it from there, we had to let it down through the woods and a field to a lower road. Apropos the tyre, this was in the early days of solid tyres, some of which could not stand the friction of tyre and road plus weight, which caused the interior of the type to become liquid.

'Solid tyres on their steel rims were pressed off the wheels by hydraulic presses at the tyre depôts and the new ones pressed on under great pressure. The tyres were smooth, whilst the contact area with the road was very

small, consequently the grip on the road on soft or wet ground was very poor.

'one of the problems with the Sentinels, of course, was raising steam in the morning. This meant lighting the fire, using South Wales Steam Coal, at least one hour before starting time. Also, at knocking-off time the firebars were dropped to clear the clinker or let out the fire, and then the bunker had to be loaded with from 5 to 10 cwt of coal. This meant a long day, yet the men did not complain all that much. I think that it is partly because, once clear of the garage, a driver, even today, is his own boss. He knows what he is doing and where he is going, and it gives him a feeling of adventure.

'One thing about these old steam vehicles was their extreme reliability, even so long ago. This can be seen today, when the present-day diesel engines on the railways still do not come up to the old steam railway engines. Timekeeping was far more reliable than today, whilst their drivers and firemen took great pride in the appearance of their engines.

'What killed the steam wagon was the 1933 Road & Traffic Act when, because of keen competition, the railways were losing traffic to the roads. The government stepped in and raised the taxation of road vehicles

according to their unladen weight and carrying capacity. The steamers lost out in these two things, as they were, of course, very heavily built in addition to carrying a lot of water and fuel that cut into the payload allowance. The local station master was very pleased as he said that "this would put Roberts off the road"!'

Tecwyn Roberts thinks that it was a great pity that the government of the day killed off the vehicles able to run on home produced fuel. He and his father attempted to make a living with their modern Super Sentinel but in time were forced to switch over to light petrol vehicles. These they found ideal for the narrow and twisty Welsh lanes where access to farms and sites was often difficult. They bought a number of Bedford 1½ and 2 tonners (two of which had Muir-Hill third axle conversions) following satisfactory service from a British-assembled 1930 Chevrolet 1½ tonner. The only real trouble with the early Bedfords, Tecwyn Roberts remembers, was that their brakes were very poor and required constant readjustment until hydraulic brakes (as found on contemporary Dodges) were adopted. They also ran a 1933 C type Morris-Commercial and two 1930 Guy 3 ton tippers. These Guys were part of a fleet that had been used for major roadworks and tunnel digging near

This 1950 Thornycroft five tonner had a Thornycroft diesel engine and was well liked by the drivers though rather underpowered.

The Thornycroft again with a massive load of straw bales. It is shown with driver John Roberts outside Ruthin station, which closed in 1968 after years of competition with local road hauliers.

Penmaenmawr and were acquired when the contract ended. Their engines are remembered as being rather small and their low geared worm axles gave them adequate power but little speed or performance. However, the pride of their fleet in 1935 was a 5-6 ton Sentinel Garner six wheeler, bought new because of their satisfaction with the steam Sentinels.

Sentinel had taken over the Birmingham Garner firm to cushion the effect of taxation on their steamer sales and Tecwyn Roberts remembers that his lorry was well made and fitted with an Austin 20 6 cyl engine:

'A very good engine but underpowered for the weight it had to carry.

'In 1937 we purchased a 5 ton 4 wheeler, now named 'Garner' only because Sentinel had sold their Garner division to a group of London businessmen. It was fitted with an American Waukesha 6 cyl engine and we specified a lower axle ratio to cope with the terrain around Ruthin. This turned out to be an extremely reliable vehicle for the delivery of feeding stuffs and fertilisers to upland farms. Appertaining to this type of work by road, it only commenced in the late 1920s and 1930s whilst there was considerable objection from the railway companies, which culminated in the Road & Rail Traffic Act of 1933. This came about because during the 1920s and early 1930s the railway companies had become worried by the amount of traffic lost, especially long distance, to road haulage. In addition, the general slump at that time made things worse. They were successful in getting the Government to introduce the Act in 1933 which compelled road hauliers to be licensed, maintain their vehicles in good order, restrict their driving hours and keep within the condition of a licence according to the type of work carried out. A haulier would automatically be granted a licence for the total unladen weight of the vehicles which the operator had on the road in 1931. This date, unfortunately, coincided with the general slump in business, so that a haulier might have laid aside a number of vehicles owing to lack of work.

'An A licence allowed a haulier purely and simply to carry any type of goods to any part of the country. A B licence, for one who had a business of his own, anywhere but goods for hire and reward according to agreed conditions of type of goods or radius mileage. A C licence was for private use, allowing a firm to carry its own goods to wherever it wanted, but not for "hire or reward".

'Traffic courts were set up to deal with applications for licences, the A licence being valid for 5 years and the B licence for 2 years.

'The railways soon clamped down on all applications by objecting on all occasions, so that a precedent was set, based on the Enston Case, whereby not only did an applicant have to prove that "the traffic was there to be moved, but also that it could not be moved by any other means", a very difficult thing to do. The Enston firm was based near us in Mold, North Wales, and this case became famous all over the country, as it was continually quoted by the railway companies against all similar applications.

'The road hauliers got together to form an association - The Road Haulage Association. Information as to applications, court times and places, etc, were published in 'Applications & Decisions' or ADs. A committee was formed, comprising members of the RHA and the railways to discuss beforehand the objections received by an applicant, to see if it was possible to remove objections, both from hauliers and the railways. If an agreement was reached, the Traffic Commissioners would be informed that objections to the application as it stood would be withdrawn, or that the applicant had agreed to rather less conditions than applied for. In such cases, the Commissioner would grant the application according to the agreed conditions.

'The railways managed to whittle down the A licences from being a carry-all/go-everywhere licence to the

A 1955 Guy six tonner with Homalloy cab that was acquired by Tecwyn Roberts in 1959. It had a Perkins P6 and was slow but sure. The driver is W H Walker.

One of the fleet's last new vehicles was this 1960 Thames Trader seven tonner. With are Elwyn Jones, Bob Hughes [driver] and Bob Evans. The Traders had lots of reserve power which encouraged some operators to overload them.

actual work carried out by the haulier applicants, whilst if he had changed the nature or area of his work the railways would object on renewal of his licence.

'Another of our problems in the 1930s came when the railways acquired vehicles to compete with us and other road hauliers, cutting prices drastically, and delivering feeding stuffs, fertilisers, etc, free of charge for the first three miles. Also, with regard to livestock, the railways had a considerable number of livestock waggons and were being hit rather badly, until they offered to collect and delivery by road for the ridiculous charge per load of two shillings and sixpence (22½ New Pence) within a certain radius! They also called out for a 'square deal'. However, in spite of all restrictions place our way, road haulage prospered as the demand increased. Thus, fortunately, there was a pool of transport available at the

beginning of the 1939-45 War to carry out essential work and also relieve the railways as depôts and rail connections were bombed'.

W H Roberts died in 1945 and as his son Tecwyn remembers, 'The following years were extremely difficult. We could not obtain new vehicles and one had to have a permit even to get on the waiting list. There was obviously a lull at the end of the war as war essential work ceased, but there was considerable maintenance work required on the roads, and various new schemes started up so we were kept busy.

'Competition began to get intensive, both as regards transport work and also in vehicle improvements. The Socialists having got in after the war, they proceeded to nationalise all vehicles for hire and reward, excluding C licences on the basis that if more than 50% of the work was over a 25-mile radius, then one was automatic-

ally taken over. If under these limits, one could choose not to be taken over and to remain within this radius. However, it was soon obvious that the railways were watching one's movements and were very ready to pounce if one transgressed. Also it was noticed that hauliers within reach were being taken over, leaving one isolated, where one had expected to be able to cooperate.

'With a change of government in 1951, the Conservatives proceeded to de-nationalise, selling vehicles with an S licence where there were buyers. Many of the old hauliers, who had been going since the 1920s, decided not to bother and took on other businesses or retired. I had, personally, purchased a local coal and haulage business which I expanded to deal with all kinds of agricultural requirements'.

The new firm ran quite a mixed fleet of vehicles - Bedford, Dodge, Guy, Austin, Thornycroft and Ford. The early post-war Bedfords and Fords suffered a lot of rear spring breakages and Tecwyn Roberts recalls that the Bedford gearboxes did not last as well as the Dodges', often wearing out their selectors. The Bedfords were also more prone to crown wheel/pinion and half shaft breakages.

The Guy in the fleet was a 1955 six tonner, acquired in 1959, with Homalloy cab and Perkins P6 diesel which always seemed to lack power compared with a new Thames Trader seven tonner bought that year. This was diesel powered and very compact for its capacity, which made it ideal for narrow lanes and gateways. It had such a reserve of power that some operators in the area ran their Traders with as much as 11 tons on board.

After a lifetime in road haulage, Tecwyn Roberts retired in 1966 just as A, B and C licences were abolished and still more Ministry of Trasnport regulations took their place governing braking efficiency, power to weight ratio and, of course, ever stricter testing. Now aged 74, he says he is glad to be out of the rat race but has many happy memories of his 40-plus years in the business.

Forgotten Coachbuilders No.1
ROBBINS *of* PUTNEY

**Countless garages and motor dealers became involved in WD surplus
vehicles after the Great War. Most are long since forgotten
but a few that could actually improve their purchases with the aid
of good workshops and bodyshops lived on. One of these
was Robbins of Putney, still well known in the car retail trade.
MIKE WORTHINGTON-WILLIAMS looks back on
their lorry involvement fifty to sixty years ago.**

IN our *VINTAGE CAR ANNUAL*
Mike Worthington-Williams looked at
the Robbins family's involvement with
eighty years of car maintenance,
repairs and sales. For some sixty years
the business has prospered under the
name of its founder, S T Robbins, and
today concentrates on Rolls-Royce
and Bentley cars.

Stanley Thomas Robbins was at one
time equally involved with lorries,
having acted as a vehicle procurement
officer in the Great War when the

shortage of military transport became
apparent and civilian lorries in good
condition had to be found at short
notice. This experience proved
invaluable when he began to deal in
WD surplus trucks from premises in
Upper Richmond Road, Putney. After
all, everything depended on being able
to sort out the bargains amongst the
thousands of lorries being sold from
such dumps as Slough. As many of the
lorries needed rebodying for their new
civilian duties, Stanley Robbins, by

now in his forties, set up a coachworks
under the supervision of an ex-
Maudslay craftsman named Sid
Hickman. Amongst the various
carpenters, joiners and labourers were
two highly skilled coachpainters,
Messrs Booth and Mathews who, until
the arrival of cellulose painting in the
late twenties, would apply up to
22 coats of paint and varnish by hand

**One of the more unusual makes to be rebodied
and overhauled after war service was this
American Selden.**

Before starting his own firm in 1921, Stanley Robbins was General Manager of the St George's Motor Co of Kensington, who built the body on this c1910 Dennis.

to each body, flattening each coat in between with 'wet and dry' and, finally, cuttlefish bones.

One of Robbins' first refurbished and rebodied lorries had been a Daimler, converted from a car, which he had used for moving his family and possessions when he set up in business on his own in the early twenties. Later he converted a Talbot for use as a works lorry. For some ten years lorries played a very important part in the firm's affairs, but as commercial bodybuilders grew in size and complexity, the smaller specialists found their hand methods too expensive and slowly dropped out of the market.

In Robbins' case, car body and mechanical repairs more than made up for this loss, though a brief return to it was made in the Second World War when mobile canteens and ambulances had to be built urgently.

In this selection of pictures we show just a few of the commercial vehicles with which Robbins' were involved in their early years.

The lorry built on a c1912 Daimler car chassis which served as works hack for S T Robbins in the early twenties.

Another civilianised lorry, in this case a three ton Albion. To obtain the gleaming finish, the coachpainters sprinkled used tea leaves on the floor to minimise dust.

23

Stanley Robbins was a personal friend of Alexander Duckham, and was one of the oil magnate's first retailers, so not surprisingly Robbins supplied many of Duckham's early delivery vehicles, like this RC Commer.

25

A fleet of Hallfords bought by Stanley Robbins at the War Disposal Boards Slough depôt. Robbins' keen eye for mechanical detail enabled him to avoid many of the average hauliers' pitfalls at these sales.

A typical 3 ton Subsidy Dennis of the Great War awaiting a new home at S T Robbins.

A relatively unusual make to be bought at an ex-WD sale and re-bodied as a van was this De Dion-Bouton one tonner.

One of the earliest new lorries to be supplied, cabbed and bodied by Stanley Robbins' own firm was this attractive GMC.

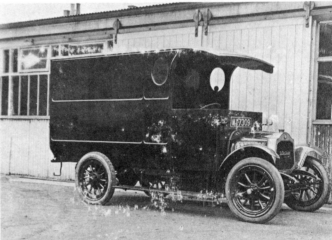

An unusual gown van body with side entrance and enclosed cab built by Robbins on a Chevrolet chassis about 1924.

A Robbins van body on a new chassis, in this case a *c*1926 Albion SB24 40 cwt Subsidy model.

After extensive rebodying and mechanical work at Putney, it is hard to decide what this ex-WD chassis started life as. The rear wheels are typical fitments to Talbot and Star staff cars, the extended dumbirons suggest American origin and the radiator badge appears to be from a Leyland.

By the mid-twenties Robbins was becoming less involved with bodywork and the General Strike in 1926 convinced him that the future lay in car sales and repairs. This Chevrolet may have been one of the last with a Robbins body or may simply have been supplied by him.

The lettering on this Austin Twelve-based van was painted freehand by Bert Mathews, using a brush in his right hand and a small paint pot and thimble in his left, the thimble being used for pressing air bubbles out of the bristles.

This beautifully sign-written truck set its owner back £325, a price which included licence, tax, insurance and spare wheel. Note the mixture of Dunlop Cord front and MacIntosh NAP semi-pneumatic rear tyres.

Almost unrecognisable as an ex-WD AEC three tonner, this truck supplied by Robbins about 1930 has such modern refinements as an enclosed cab and pneumatic tyres, though no electric lights.

WHERE DO WE START

**How does the old lorry enthusiast and historian find out about
long ago facts and obscure manufacturers or models?
In this article we attempt to give some of the answers
and describe some of the sources
and the innumerable pitfalls that accompany them.**

NUMEROUS problems face the
seeker after motor history and particularly the lorry enthusiast. The industry
has been poorly chronicled over at any
rate the first seventy years of its life
and it is now very difficult to separate
fact from fiction or to get a balanced
view of what early road haulage or
lorry manufacture was really like. One
of the biggest problems is in putting
different lorry makers into perspec-
tive.

Everyone knows who the giants were
in the twenties and thirties, but where
do the others fit in - the Guys, the

Garners, the Singers and the Vulcans?
There were no SMMT statistics as
there are today to show each rival's
month-by-month sales (themselves
open to misinterpretation in the future
if our successors forget that they show
only registrations not total production; thus Foden always looks much
smaller than, say, ERF because its off
road dumptrucks are not recorded
and no account of either firm's
substantial exports are, of course,
made). Over the years in *OLD
MOTOR*, and now in *VINTAGE
LORRY ALBUM*, we have endeav-

oured to get at least a rough idea of
certain manufacturers' production
figures and have, for example, been
able to confirm the tiny scale of the
Shefflex operation and the tremendous decline of Maudslay in the
thirties preceded and followed by
much more successful decades.
Unfortunately, such statistics, by their
very nature, are random and confined
to a very small number of firms who
have either survived and kept good
records (very rare indeed) or else
whose records have survived at, say,
the National Motor Museum or some

The *Gazette* was first published in 1925 and continued in place of the earlier *AEC Service Gazette* which had been primarily for dealers. Up until 1950 the *AEC Gazette* was of 'handy pocket size'. It contained articles about AEC operators, new vehicles, recent deliveries, service notes plus the usual component advertisements, and was well illustrated.

Early editions had a colour drawing on the cover which was repeated for several issues. This later gave way to a photograph of an AEC vehicle, and this was changed each issue. The size was enlarged up to about A4 in 1951 and a slight change of title came with the acquisition of Crossley and Maudslay [*ACV Gazette*]; earlier, during the Daimler amalgamation, it had been *ADC Gazette*. Foreign language editions were issued to coincide with overseas sales campaigns, for AEC were, at one time, particularly strong in many Spanish and Portuguese speaking countries where they were marketed as ACLO.

One of the best known of the manufacturers' publications, *The Leyland Journal* first appeared in 1935 and continued until 1970 except during the war period. It has appeared in both monthly and bi-monthly forms, presumably depending on the fortunes of the company. Early editions always carried the same front cover design, but during the late 1940s this gave way to a fresh colour illustration each issue. The magazine carried a lot of advertising by component suppliers, but there was also a fair proportion of articles on fleets, countries and operators of interest to enthusiasts, as well as new vehicle sections, service notes and good illustrations.

As Albion and Scammell joined the group so their products came to be mentioned in the publication; and the various other constituent companies' journals were phased out.

library (as in the case of the Dorman engine records - which helps to give an idea of the relative importance of Dorman users, but is of little value in the case of firms using other makes of engine and no use at all if they only bought odd Dormans, like Austin and Willys-Overland, presumably for evaluation).

It should be possible to get a more accurate idea of relative sales positions by studying registration records and much valuable work was done in this field by psv enthusiasts before registration records were dispersed to libraries, individuals and the Swansea VLO. In many areas there were vast gaps in registration records, often attributable to the last war, so at best this method could only give accurate details over short time spans in particular areas. Unfortunately, most of the published material relates principally to buses and coaches, at any rate from the days before widespread interest in lorries. What tends to show up from this research is that Dennis, AEC, Leyland, Thornycroft, etc, were front ranking across the nation, but others had strong pockets of popularity which could easily be missed if the records for, say, Huddersfield (where perhaps the local make Karrier reigned supreme) had

Recently ceased publication [1977], *The Bedford Transport Magazine* took on this title soon after the first Bedford trucks began to appear in 1931, for it was previously known as *The Chevrolet Magazine*. Actually, the change of name occurred gradually over several issues. With such a widespread dealership, the *BTM* was almost as prolific as the Bedford trucks themselves, and it was probably the most easily acquired manufacturer's magazine.

During the 1930s the cover carried some particularly colourful drawings of Bedford trucks at work in a wide variety of locations. Contents included the usual advertisements, but also good illustrated articles on Bedford users, new deliveries, service notes and general guidance on new vehicle legislation.

Like its contemporaries, the post-war issues had a photograph on the cover, this later being in colour. Always a good source of information and vehicle photographs, the passing of *The Bedford Transport Magazine* was caused by the high costs involved in publishing and printing.

not survived. From the W&G story in *VLA 1*, we were able to show that the firm was very strong in South Wales, thanks to records kept by Chris Taylor who lives in the area, and we know they were successful in London and the East Midlands, but who is to say that they were not briefly the number one light commercial in Norfolk or the

north of Scotland? - frankly we do not know and have no means of checking.

In many cases lorry firms had (and indeed still have) very few distributors and inevitably the strongest sales were nearest to the depôts of these. Several of these firms still survive, even if the manufacturers for which they held the franchise disappeared long ago. Sometimes they can give an idea of sales, but more often it is just an impression such as 'oh yes, we did very well with Stars, we sold them to all the local livestock customers'.

So how do we find out the relative scale of manufacturers and gather other details such as dates of model introductions and technical specifications? Well, the answer is partly from old time employees, partly from contemporary sales literature, and partly from the transport press of the day. The first line is the most interesting but inevitably the most unreliable, the second is much better but beset with problems such as the fact that the material is often not dated or has an undecipherable printer's date code and may or may not show the

first of a particular model or sometimes even a prototype, which differs in subtle ways from what actually entered production. Sometimes catalogues were prepared for vehicles that never saw the light of day, or else specifications were sent out to the compilers of buyers' guides for vehicles that never entered production, like a mysterious 35hp 30 cwt AEC of 1929 which appears in Stone and Cox or the little Leyland shown in *Modern Motors* in 1922 that looked like nothing before or since but was briefly unveiled at Olympia in 1923.

So that leaves us with the technical press which, unfortunately in many ways, is the least satisfactory of all the avenues of research. The trouble here is that investigative journalism was frowned upon until *Truck* came on the scene and magazines until quite

The magazine of Morris-Commercials was rather slimmer than the Bedford magazine, although it did put on a little weight during its later life in post-war years. It contained the usual details of new models, fleet operators, recent deliveries, service notes and company news, together with advertisements by supporting parts and servicing suppliers.

After the forming of British Motor Corporation, a new *BMC User* magazine appeared, but this died after the BLMC merger. The early issues of the magazine have coloured drawings on the cover but some were not very accurately drawn. Later editions carried black and white photographs, but the widespread use of colour photography did not embrace the cover of *Transport Efficiency* before it disappeared, along with Morris-Commercial vehicles.

Absorbed into *Commercial Motor* in 1973, *Commercial Vehicles* underwent many changes during its career. Originally the restricted circulation publication of the Commercial Motor Users Association, the early editions of *CMUA Journal* were made up of reports, news and information for CMUA members, the CMUA being the trade association for commercial vehicle operators, not general carriers or haulage contractors. The Road Haulage Association was [and still is] the body for haulage contractors, and they publish *The Roadway*.

The first change of title was to that of *Commercial Vehicle Users Journal* when it became available for general sale, this being shortened to *Commercial Vehicles* in 1955. Another change took place in 1966 when the format was changed to almost square. It was eventually acquired by IPC, who made it 'controlled circulation' [free to eligible readers] and finally absorbed it into *Commercial Motor*. For a time in the sixties and seventies, a very useful sister publication, *Commercial Vehicles Overseas*, was produced and all have the advantage of good quality paper.

Comparatively unknown to lorry enthusiasts, *The World's Carriers* started out in 1904 as a monthly and lasted to the mid-sixties. Some of the very early editions review the operations of contemporary carriers whether they be removals, job masters, shipping, warehousing or bonded carmen. Although never profusely illustrated, photographs of pair-horse vans soon gave way to those of early Leylands, Bernas, Thornycrofts and other motor vehicles during the teens as a special Motor Section was added.

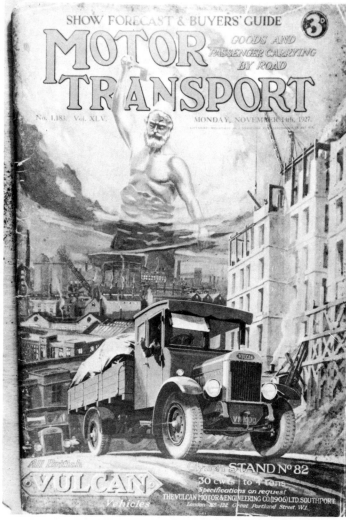

The currently published weekly had its origins way back in the early days of motoring, for it was originally the Industrial Vehicle Section of *The Autocar*. It first appeared as a separate magazine in 1905 as *Motor Traction*, and continued with this title until 1921, when it became *Motor Transport*, though still in the original magazine format. A new departure occurred in 1932 when it took on the larger form of a newspaper, and continues in this guise today.

Naturally, early editions of the magazine are rich in reference material about commercial vehicles, and contain good articles on vehicle operation, new models, large fleets and news of the period. The magazine was well illustrated and often special numbers appeared, particularly at Show times.

The change to the larger newspaper format brought certain changes, particularly in the number and quality of illustrations. Like another large size contemporary, *Modern Transport*, copies were difficult to store and became very brittle over the course of time.

recently tended to publish edited versions of roughly what motor manufacturers sent them. To an extent this still happens and in *Commercial Motor* or *Motor Transport* you often see press release photos with what appear to be only lightly edited captions as supplied by the manufacturer. If this still happens it is little wonder that in the uncritical days of the teens or twenties the firm that was best at sending out nice

pictures of its products with interesting stories to support them would get more coverage than firms that did not employ a new-fangled 'publicist' and could hardly turn out enough chassis to meet demand anyway. Thus, there are some quite important lorries which seldom, if ever, appeared in the news pages whilst there are others, like Gilford and Garner, who were never out of them.

Gilford, in particular, was a triumph of marketing and, though important in the psv field, its contribution to trucking must have been minimal. One cannot help but be drawn to the conclusion that the substantial amount they, and indeed Garner, spent on advertising had something to do with their regular editorial mentions, even if only quite innocently. After all, if the editor saw a page of Leyland advertising and a page of Gilford advertising in each of his issues he would be reminded of their 'importance' and would look favourably on their press releases, whilst Pagefield, who virtually never advertised, and who probably were equally lax about sending out photographs, were very much out of the editor's mind and, frequently, were even left out of buyers' guides. It is,

after all, human nature to go for the easiest course and a London-based and probably understaffed magazine could hardly be blamed for not wanting to send a photographer all the way to Wigan when there were things happening nearer to home. One sometimes wonders if early editorial staff did not have a finger in various manufacturing pies and I have always suspected that the reason the Coventry made Lotis van of veteran days got so many mentions is that the Sturmey of its maker Sturmey Motors was none other than Henry Sturmey of Iliffe and Sons, the publishers of *Autocar* and *Motor Traction*!

A random count in a transport magazine today of photographs of new vehicles shows how very unrepresentative of what actually is being sold they are. After all, the vast majority of trucks sold in Britain in 1980 are Fords, Leylands, Bedfords and Dodges with, way below them, fairly equal numbers of Volvos, Fodens, ERFs, Seddon-Atkinsons and, below them, a whole assortment of Britiah and imported makes. Yet in five random magazines I have just examined there are no Volvos shown editorially, no Dodges and the same number of DAFs as Leylands or

COMMERCIAL MOTOR

Registered as a Newspaper.
Entered as second-class matter at
New York, N.Y., Post Office.

Leyland

OLYMPIA

GRAND HALL	EMPIRE HALL
STAND 73	STAND 166

Probably the best known of the transport weeklies, *The Commercial Motor* **started out in 1905 and has continued in more or less the same size ever since. Cover designs have changed several times, and in recent years the arrangement, presentation and illustrations have undergone violent changes.**

It is a good source of reference for old vehicles, for it has contained well illustrated reports on Shows, large fleet operations, new vehicles and technical reviews. For very many years the Road Tests were of particular interest to modellers for they included elevational drawings of the vehicle under test.

Fords. Even Stonefield comes in for two mentions whereas Land-Rover, which must outsell Stonefield by many thousands to one, does not figure at all. Foreign vehicles illustrated outnumber British ones nearly two to one, yet in realistic sales terms the proportions should be more than reversed.

It is, perhaps, hardly surprising, therefore, in the far less commercially minded days of long ago, when editors did not expect their staff to treat press releases critically, and were on close terms with many manufacturers (just as they are today) that news content was far less balanced than today. A quick skim through the illustration index to *Commercial Motor* under lorries or wagons in 1935, 1925 and 1915 perhaps helps to show what I mean. In 1915 the only firms to get more than one specific photograph included (by this I don't mean general views of convoys, etc) are Albion and Commer, both with 9, Pierce-Arrow, Napier and Thornycroft with 5, Acason, Foden, Karrier, Leyland and Star each with 4, Dennis, Garford, Garner, Maudslay, McCurd, Palladium and Straker-Squire with 3 and Guy, Laycock, Kelly-Springfield and Scout each with 2. Admittedly, the index is not exhaustive, but where are AEC, Daimler and Lacre, to mention but 3? The inclusion of Laycock is fair as it was a new design and *Commercial Motor* can hardly be blamed for not knowing that it was to be stillborn, but why four Acasons or three of that

other American design (admittedly newly arrived), the Garner?

1925 puts Dennis way ahead of all the others in terms of photographs and probably reflects a true picture of the success of the Guildford firm. Next to it comes Ford (light vehicles always seem to get the thin end of the wedge) then Guy, who inexplicably are ahead of Leyland, Thornycroft, Albion, Vulcan and Karrier. Garner and Berliet both do disproportionately well with 4 and 5 pictures respectively, and everyone else scrapes in with one or two illustrations (or, in the case of Straker-Squire and a few other well-known firms, none).

Ten years later it is AEC that heads the league (at any rate in terms of lorry illustrations) with Armstrong-Saurer second, Morris-Commercial third, Leyland, Commer and Thornycroft tying for fourth and Albion, Crossley, Bedford, Dennis, ERF, Foden, Ford, Garner, Guy, Scammell and Vulcan well up with the front runners. Now this must surely give an extremely distorted view as, whilst Armstrong-Saurer was very strong at the heavy 'glamour' end of the market, its sales can only have been in hundreds annually. Crossley hardly had any lorry success in the thirties, except with military vehicles, so it is lucky to be represented, and for ERF to be better covered than Ford, Foden, Dodge, Guy, Karrier, Atkinson, Halley and dozens more seems a little surprising, even if it was to be an important brand.

It plainly all comes back to what is 'in the news' and in lorry terms 'in the news' means what the manufacturers thought was worth taking a picture of and sending off to the trade press. Obviously a firm that brought out regular new models had more to be covered than one that went on perfecting an old design for many years, as was (and indeed still is) common in the heavy vehicle industry.

Reviews of new models long ago in contemporary lorry magazines are notoriously unrevealing, frequently not even mentioning the make of proprietary engine, gearbox or axles fitted, and giving little more than dimensions and very vague uncritical observations. The one area where facts should abound is road tests, but again these, until recently, have been little more than waffle. In the twenties and thirties they were full of generalisations and gave a prospective purchaser or a later historian little opportunity to compare them with rival makes, except in bald facts like weights, dimensions, turning circle and gear ratios and, when they became more sophisticated, fuel consumption as well. Looking at a few random tests, I see that the 1935 Vulcan 2 tonner had brakes whose 'retarding force (was) directly proportional to the driver's efforts' - surprise, surprise - and which had an easy gearchange, it being 'unnecessary accurately to gauge the relative speeds of the meshing pinions'. No explanation for this phenomenon is given, so it is a matter of conjecture whether it had constant mesh, synchromesh or what. One final point - 'By an arrangement inside the bonnet, heating of the cab is largely avoided', which could mean almost anything.

A test of a Ford V8 showed only 40 per cent brake efficiency, but apparently its operator was more concerned with avoiding 'a violence of application that might have harmful effects on tyre wear, or prove likely to accelerate depreciation', and had adjusted the servo accordingly! The V8 engine was found to be 'very accelerative' but no effort was made to explain whether it was a worthwhile development for lorries or just a gimmick.

An AEC Monarch Mark II was 'a triumph of engineering skill' with a very 'responsive oil engine', 'first class brakes', and steering 'in view of the weight of the machine .... not unduly heavy'.

The Studebaker Leopard was a very skimpy looking three tonner which had somehow lost 8 cwt when compared with its predecessor, about which *Commercial Motor* made the uncritical observation - 'the Studebaker reputation for durability is too enviable for the manufacturers to risk jeopardising it by diminishing the lasting qualities of a new product'. Regarding its performance, *Commercial Motor* made the following rather unscientific comment: 'Along the gently rising approach to (Brockley) Hill we accelerated up to 32 mph. In doing this the driver of the vehicle refrained from changing into top gear, thereby probably reaching the foot of the 1:8½ section at a higher speed than would have otherwise been the case, and ...ing an advantage which, ...erefore, ...ust not be wholly accredited to the machine'. Why not - was the driver also pedalling furiously?!

One could go on *ad infinitum* showing the rather unsatisfactory nature of the information to be gleaned from pre-war road tests which, even if not very objective, were at least unbiased, unlike the manufacturers' own magazines that were proliferating at the time. We show the covers of a few of these of various eras and, in passing, must say that they

prove a useful source of material as they tend to be fairly specific about what had actually been changed in new models. They even sometimes give servicing advice that hints at past difficulties with particular models, as in the *AEC Gazette*, when they explain the poor reputation of their former Tylor engines of the Great War period.

Obviously the answer to a recorder of lorry history is a carefully trodden path between all the sources mentioned here, aided by an ability to read between the lines with the benefit of hindsight and, most important of all, to be able to tap other enthusiasts' or one-make clubs' specific research. Hopefully, this will be a function of *VINTAGE LORRY ALBUM*, putting us and other readers in touch with experts on particular makes or else with people who have made a special

study of such fields as municipal vehicles, tankers, and the many other spheres in Britain and abroad where lorries have played an important rôle.

Many of the well known, and some of the lesser known vehicle manufacturers have produced their own magazines. Some have continued for very many years and attracted much attention for their professionalism. Others have made brief, sporadic appearances and then disappeared from view. A few more were made generally available and had a cover price, while most were distributed to dealers and customers and the trade only. Some were quite easy to acquire while others were almost impossible to obtain, unless you could get on the mailing list or had an 'inside' contact.

By no means an exhaustive list, here are a few that have come our way over the years: *Ford Times*, *Challenge* [Ford], *Payload* [Austin], *BMC User*, *Sidelights* [BMC drivers], *Berliet Times*, *Karrier Gazette*, *Sentinel Transport News*, *Armstrong-Saurer Bulletin*, *Transportation* [Goodyear], *GMC News*, *Chevrolet Magazine*, *HELECS News*, *FWD News*, *Foden News*, *Chassis* [ERF], *Rangeability* [Atkinson], *The Atkinson*.

As well as supplying many of the military ambulances and twin shaft lorries for the 1914-18 War some of the Austin 30hp Colonial car chassis were adapted as armoured cars. A total of 480 were made and several went to Russia. They weighed 3¾ tons and could achieve 45 mph.

A PICTORIAL SURVEY

For years one of Britain's major car makers, Austin, had a love-hate relationship with lorries until it conceived a design to combat Bedford and the other mass producers in 1939. ARTHUR INGRAM has been looking at Austins over the years and now shows and describes some of the landmarks and the gradual absorption of its designs in first BMC and then Leyland

NOW that the Austin name has all but disappeared from the commercial vehicle market, it is a convenient time to take a look back over the past 70 years or so and trace the rather chequered career of the marque.

Although the Austin name has plenty of followers in the car field and the light van variants are well remembered, their heavier trucks have almost passed into oblivion since the birth of the BMC partnership and the later British Leyland amalgamation.

Not that Austin have been responsible for any really heavy trucks at all, for their range always tended to be in the 'middleweight' class of, say, 2 to 5 tons, although towards the height of

The first Austin commercials were produced in a variety of sizes and were unusual in having forward control layout with the driver seated over the T-head power unit. Many used Austin car components, like this 1908 15 cwt van chassis, also commonly used for taxicab work.

About this time, the first Austin ambulances were delivered and these were mounted on the car chassis and equipped with 20hp engines.

The next phase in the commercial vehicle story relates to Herbert Austin's revolutionary 2/3 ton truck, the first of which was built in December 1912, and when introduced to the motoring press in February 1913 caused something of a stir. The design owed nothing to contemporary British practice, for the sloping bonnet and scuttle radiator were more in keeping with French designs while the lattice type chassis side members pierced by the twin drive shafts were unique in lorry chassis layout. Other features included a straight front beam axle, engine angled in frame to achieve a straight drive line in the unladen position, differential behind gearbox, twin crown wheel and pinion drives and double spring rear suspension.

It was perhaps fortuitous for Herbert Austin that World War I was not long in coming, for the twin shaft lorry was just a little too revolutionary for some and it failed to sell well, that is, of course, until the military tried one out and found it to their liking. Quite a number were shipped to Russia to help the Czar, but even this went sour, for while about 1000 were waiting at Longbridge during 1917 the Revolution took place and so the order was not completed.

Even less well known was the 5 ton version of the twin shaft model, for it is reputed that only two were completed, one for the Midland Railway and the other retained on works transport. The 5 tonner had a 111 x 152mm four cylinder engine rated at 30hp while the smaller 2/3 ton model was powered by the 95 x 127mm unit rated at 20hp, which lived on until 1929.

Although the twin shaft models were not built after 1917 - they had enough in stock - they were on offer up to 1922 and total sales amounted to some 2000 in all.

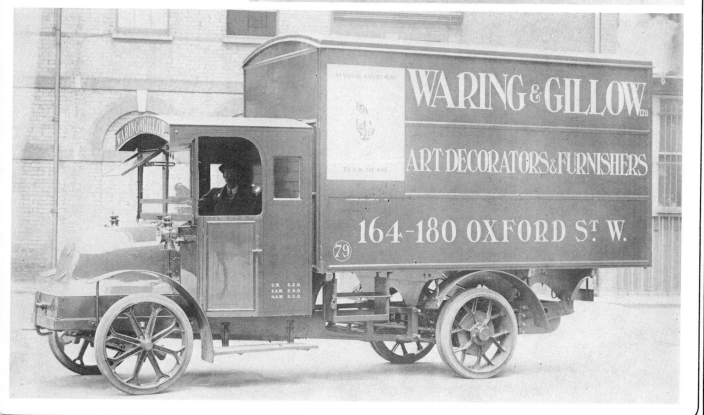

their popularity a straight 7 tonner was listed and artic and multi-axle versions did give higher weights.

It seems that the best remembered Austin trucks are those that took the road to war in both conflicts, but that is not so remarkable for war often tends to bring out the best in people -- or so we're told! The 1914-1918 War helped establish the peculiar twin-shaft model, while Hitler's war enabled the ubiquitous K2 to make its mark in truck history.

Much of the popularity of the Austin name in the field of light vans can be attributed to the famous Seven car in the twenties and thirties, although due regard must be made for their many ambulances on the larger 20hp chassis in the early days, and the more recent Three-Way design of the fifties, together with the once popular

There was just one other true Austin lorry chassis before 1939. This was of 30 cwt capacity and was announced at the 1919 Commercial Motor Show. It was powered by a 3600cc 35 bhp Austin 20 engine and had a conventional front radiator similar to the contemporary Austin Farm and industrial tractor. One noticeable feature of the type was the external steering box. Probably in order to make the machine more marketable at such a difficult trading time as the post-war depression, the rated capacity was increased to 2 tons, but all to no avail, for production ceased in 1921.

Their one-engine policy [20hp] soon had to be expanded and the result was the famous Seven and Twelve. The van version of the Austin Seven appeared in 1923, rated as a 2½ cwt load carrier, and soon found buyers in all types of trades which could afford mechanical power in place of the errand boy on his bicycle or box trike. By 1931 improvements in the Seven design were reflected in the van version being uprated to 5 cwt capacity. Here we see a 1930 example with a craze of the time - a fabric body.

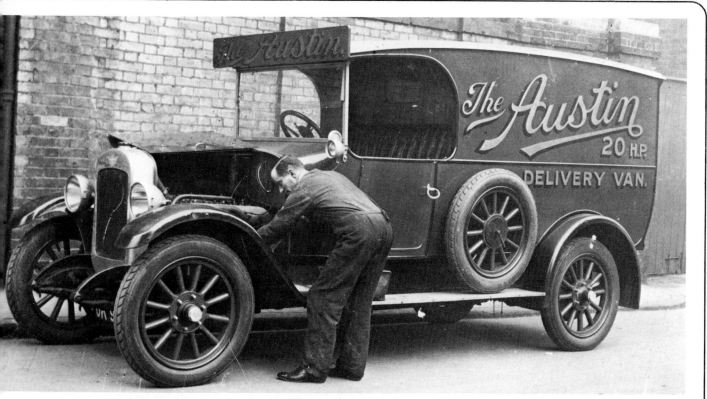

A40 vans and their later counterparts.
   More recent history of both trucks and light vans is less clear-cut because of the on/off partnership with Morris and the final absorption into BL with all the name swapping that has followed.

Other car based models included the Heavy Twelve, introduced in 1921, and the stalwart 20hp, shown here, both of which formed the basis for vans plus the ambulance side of the business. The Twenty could carry 16 cwt and was produced until 1929.

Many of the early designs of ambulance were austere in the extreme, particularly those produced for the war effort, which were merely conversions of car chassis/front ends on a limited budget. These vehicles came to be termed 'temporary' ambulances, whereas the better equipped and finished vehicles were termed 'permanent'. Many of the ambulances were factory advertised, although gradually some bodybuilders took up their construction wholeheartedly and made a speciality of them.
   The Austin Heavy Twelve chassis shown here was rated at 10 cwt capacity and continued to be offered right up to 1939 although the engine underwent an increase in stroke in October 1926 when its capacity was increased from 1660 to 1861cc. It was termed the Twelve Four from 1933.

The range of vans was extended in 1930 by the addition of two six cylinder engined chassis - one of 3.1 litres and the other of 3.4 litres. By 1933 the van listing was nothing short of impressive - 5 cwt 4 cylinder Seven, 7 cwt 4 cylinder Ten Four, 10 cwt 4 cylinder Twelve Four, 10 cwt 6 cylinder Light Twelve Six, 10 cwt 6 cylinder Sixteen, 15 cwt Twenty [now 6 cylinder and 23.4hp] and the 7/10 cwt 4 cylinder Light Twelve Four! But this was not all, for soon after there was an optional engine for the Light Twelve Six and one had a choice of a pair of sixes with capacities of 1496cc or 1711cc. From this multitude we show a 1933 12/6 van with unusual body.

With a growing emphasis on municipal ambulance production, higher powered chassis were produced - the Sixteen, Eighteen and Twenty, all six cylinder models using the 1711cc, 2510cc and 3400cc engines. A four cylinder [3476cc] engine was used in the smaller Twelve ambulance chassis.

It was obviously quite wasteful to catalogue such a wide range of similar chassis and towards the end of the 1930s there was a slimming down of the commercial range until just three van and two ambulance models remained, but even these five models had their individual engines. These 1936 Eighteen vans were bodied by Goddard of Oadby and laughingly known as the Gas Department's hearses!

1939 saw the introduction of a completely new lorry chassis in the middleweight class with payloads of 30 cwt, 2 tons and 3 tons. There is no doubt that Austin had watched the market carefully during the thirties and witnessed the phenomenal growth of Bedford alongside Ford, Commer and Morris, plus the imports from America such as Dodge, Reo, Diamond T, Studebaker and International. The other aspect of the Austin return to lorry production was that they had the foresight to realise that the impending war would mean a very big demand for military equipment and all that it entailed. Of course many others had watched what was going on in Europe and the term 'shadow factory' took on a more tangible form in various parts of the country.

Press reports of the launch of the new Austin range in January 1939 mentioned the wide selection of Austin-built bodywork available on the three models, and most of them came within the important 2½ ton unladen weight figure and so achieved that legal 30 mph limit. A massive extension to the Longbridge plant had been going on since 1926 at a cost of £3½m and the company was at pains to point out that their 1939 prices were half what they had been in 1922.

No sooner had the Austin range started to trickle through than the country was plunged into World War II and restrictions placed on the supply of new vehicles for civilian use. The rare 30 cwt model was produced from March 1939 to August 1941 during which time a total of 4625 were turned out. From then on, 2 ton and 3 ton chassis were produced, although, of course, there were additional types such as six wheelers and austere forward control 4x4s of military type.

Many of the wartime 2 tonners were turned out as ambulances or towing vehicles for the fire service, while the K3 3 ton 4x4s were GS trucks, the K5 3 ton 4x4 either GS or anti-aircraft portee and the K6 6x4 3 ton was issued as GS, mobile crane, breakdown truck, signals vehicle, bomb platform or bus types. Some of the wartime production did find its way into non-military rôles, the chassis being available for important civil operations against Ministry of Supply permits.

At the end of hostilities many ex-military machines were pressed into service by civilian transport firms because of the scarcity of new vehicles. When the fire service was denationalised in 1948 the K2 ATVs remained with the civilian brigades in a variety of rôles. Some of them were extensively rebuilt for a new stint of duty and remained in service for many years.

First models to appear in the post-war range were similar in appearance to the pre-war 'Birmingham Bedfords'. They were the K4 5 tonner and K2 2 tonner.

The normal control lorries were soon supplemented by the K8 25 cwt payload Three-Way van, the bodywork of which was somewhat revolutionary for the period, with loading doors on both sides and at the rear. About the same time it was announced that a new company had been set up with Crompton Parkinson to take over the electric vehicle production previously carried on under the Morrison Electric name.

In 1948 the introduction of the new styled 10 cwt van had taken place, this being based on the current Austin Devon car with ohv engine and independent front suspension.

New for 1952 was the four wheel drive Champ 5 cwt aimed at the cross-country and military spheres of operation, but it was rather short-lived, being discontinued in May 1956. But 1953 saw several changes with the introduction of the first BMC diesel engine and the adoption of the Morris Commercial LC5 1½ ton truck with 2.2 litre ohv petrol engine followed by the diesel version in December 154. The K9 medium 4x4 shown here was also introduced for military and similar markets, and the example is shown many years later with modified lighting to suit contemporary legislation.

The four model range of Austin commercials continued through 1948 and into 1949 when the truck models were restyled with the appearance of the Loadstar range called Series II. A newcomer was the export orientated A70 pick-up based on the current larger Hampshire car.

A new factory was obtained in 1950, it being situated near Longbridge, and there were improvements to the light van in 1951, but the next major step was the setting up of the British Motor Corporation in 1952 in collaboration with Morris. Resulting from this amalgamation was a slightly rationalised range of Austin and Morris-Commercial trucks, vans and engines under the BMC label, although it took some time for them to appear.

Further evidence of the Morris influence was felt in 1954 with the angular LD 1½ and 2 ton vans being available with Austin badges. Other new models included the GV5, which was the last of the A40 van variants soon to be replaced by the new A50 Cambridge range in March 1955, followed by the A55 in November 1956.

The little Austin A30 or Seven 5 cwt van was also new in August 1954, but it was to last only until October 1956 when it was uprated to become the A35 with a 948cc engine in place of the original 800cc type. One interesting and short-lived version of the A35 was the pick-up which was listed from November 1956 to November 1957.

In 1955 there came several changes of importance. The 3K, 4K and 5K models were restyled and designated Series III and were listed as 303, 403 and 503 [shown] respectively in the BMC coding for Morris badging. Both petrol and diesel engines were available and a choice of either forward or normal control layout. For the first time a new model was introduced purely as a BMC - the 701 7 tonner in an effort to gain some of that payload market acquired by Commer and Bedford with their QX and S types.

More signs of the growing integration of Austin and Morris in the shape of an Austin badged and engined Morris-Commercial two tonner. This example dates from 1958 and is still in use in Norfolk. It is a 301 type LCS, chassis number 50996.

Also in 1955 was the availability of the J type Morris Commercial 10 cwt van as the Austin JB or 101 model with the Austin 1489cc ohv engine in place of the old Morris side-valve unit. Another, slightly larger, forward control van also came onto the scene this year and is shown here - the 152 or Omnivan, known also as the J2. This shared the 1489cc ohv engine and was rated as 12/15 cwt capacity.

There was a change of heart about the 7 tonner in 1956 for, as from November, it was no longer a BMC vehicle but reverted to badging as either Austin or Morris. It was now also available as a tractor model. Our example dates from February 1956 so still has the BMC badge.

The bonneted 403 was replaced by the 14K series which, according to official literature, was a 4 tonner but with 3 tonner type frame and axles! Early in 1958 the Gipsy 4x4 with independent suspension made its debut as an entrant in the cross-country stakes where the Land-Rover had it much its own way.

In May of 1958 the Series III FC 7 tonner [702] came onto the scene with modified front end styling and the same six cylinder 105 bhp diesel as its predecessor.

In the late 1950s British Road Services designed their own style of retail delivery box van for the parcels service. A simple glassfibre hinged bonnet was provided for the benefit of servicing, and deep sliding doors made cab entry and exit much easier. A platform bodied version was produced for the Meat Cartage Department.

Into 1960 we find that the Series II Gipsy is announced with new beam axle suspension, modified steering and high ratio on four wheel drive, and in July a long wheelbase version appeared. The all new Mini 5 cwt van was introduced in January 1960 [for a change, we show a rare artic conversion], as was an uprated version of the 152 van for 16/18 cwt loads, and the new forward control van on the 7ft 2ins wheelbase chassis made an entrance just before the JB was discontinued. This new model was the J4 van which was joined by a pick-up version in the following year; payload for both models was 10/12 cwt.

Announced at the 1959 Scottish Show was the revolutionary FG type cab which was soon nicknamed the 'threepenny piece' after the twelve-sided coin of pre-decimal currency. It was an easy access forward control cab with the doors placed at about 45° to the rear and it replaced the older type forward control cab on the 1½, 2, 3 and 4 ton sizes. The normal control cab remained. The FG-cabbed 2 tonner was first introduced as the T200 with the 1½ ton model being labelled S200; the 3 ton model was also the 304 and the 4 ton the 404.

The opening of a new plant at Bathgate in Scotland was instrumental in the new cab [which is still produced today] and there was more to follow.

In November 1961 a 5 ton version of the FG chassis appeared, while in 1962 a whole new system of coding was introduced in an effort to unify the Austin and Morris systems. The new chassis symbols were based on the theory that the designation should signify the type of cab, the factory of origin and the nominal payload in hundredweights. Following this system the LD4 van introduced in March 1960 was coded LDM 20, this being the 1 ton model, while the 3 ton lorry previously known as the 304 became the FG K 60. The new forward control cab [shown here on an FFK 140 Unipower 6x4 conversion with Hendrickson bogie], introduced in November 1959, became the FF cab, the low access cab the FG, the normal control cab the WE, whilst the LD, J4, J2 or G2 [Gipsy] were applied as necessary to the van models. There were two factory origins listed: K for Longbridge or Bathgate [Austin] or M for Morris Commercial. Although the last figure in the code represented the payload in cwts, this was amended to the gross weight in respect of articulated tractor models.

1963 saw the introduction of the FH forward control truck range in place of the FF, with models in the 5, 7 and 8 ton load categories. This was very closely followed by another variation, the FJ, which appeared in August 1964 and modified versions of its cab are used today on the Bathgate Leylands.

With the change in designation in 1962, the 503 and other models with the same cab had become WE types and these were updated in 1962 as WFs with twin headlights and single piece windscreens amongst other modifications. The WF has been a consistent export earner ever since, going as far afield as China, Africa, South America or, as shown here with this WF K 120, the Middle East. The 6 tonner could have four or five speed gearboxes and 5.1 or 5.7 litre diesels and the range went right down to a 30 cwt WF K 30 with 72 bhp engine and single tyre equipment.

We are now approaching the end of our story for the mid-1960s saw two major changes of ownership in quick succession which tended to push the Austin name further into the shadows. But before that there was yet another change of chassis coding, announced in November 1967.

This revised system referred to the gross weight of the vehicle first, followed by the type. Under this new system the J4 M10 [shown] became the 190J4 and the FJK 240 was listed as 1200FJT. The gross weight is ascertainable by placing a decimal point two digits from the right and, in

the case of tractor units, the figure represented the combination weight of the outfit.

Another newcomer in 1964 was the Minimoke or runabout version of the Mini, but this was essentially a general purpose vehicle with little goods carrying application, although some special six wheel versions were built for mounting film cameras. Of course, these had 6x2 [front wheel drive] though some prototypes were built with 4x4, often achieved with two engines.

The 250JU 18/20 cwt van and pick-up was introduced early in 1967, and later in the year the rather odd looking FM with its glass fibre hood tacked on the front of a modified FG cab was added to the range. This arrangement was made to provide a full three man cab without any engine hump to prevent cross cab access, and was aimed primarily at the Post Office fleet.

The takeover by the British Motor Corporation of the Jaguar-Guy-Daimler group led to the formation of British Motor Holdings which, in 1968, joined the Leyland Motor Corporation to form the British Leyland Motor Corporation. Another bout of BMC badging took place and new models such as the EA van and the LR or Laird truck duly appeared, soon followed by the Mastiff and Boxer ranges which fall more naturally into the next chapter of BL history when, after 1970, the Austin-Morris division was formed [we show a JU model from the Austin-Morris era]. Although the Austin name lives on in this way, any form of individual identity has been gradually eroded and it is convenient to end the story just here, although no doubt many think the true Austin commercial died some time before.

SEEN & HEARD

WELL KNOWN IN AND AROUND Tenbury Wells but seldom seen much farther afield is Mr Bowkley's unusual 1918 Thornycroft four tonner .....

SEEN BY PATRICK STARK of The Bush Inn, Robeston Wathen, Pembs, whilst in Mahon, Majorca, was this c1934 Ford BB with locally built cab .....

DAVE HURLEY HAS PRESERVED a twin shaft Austin lorry chassis of the Great War period. It still has its rear drive boxes but not much else. Can anyone help him as it would be very nice to see one of these unusual vehicles running again .....

A READER IN SUSSEX is anxious to dispose of this 1950 Foden eight wheeler with the remains of a Peerless chassis on its bed. The only snag is that the Foden has an alloy body which would make even its scrap value around £1000. Enquiries can be forwarded and the reader also has a wartime Bedford OXC tractive unit for sale. He is currently restoring an attractive vintage Thornycroft van and desperately needs space .....

ROBIN BARNARD of The Grove, Seaton, Devon, is restoring a 1937 Morris-Commercial C11/30 30 cwt truck ex Corona and needs many spares and a radiator badge. He also has a Commer Q2 and knows where a 1927 Singer light lorry (probably cut down from a car) can be found in a scrapyard .....

FROM SCOTLAND COMES NEWS that Andrew Scott of Myreton Garage, Tealing by Dundee, is rescuing several interesting early post-war vehicles, including Maudslay Mogul III and Mammoth Major, Dennis Jubilant, 1947 Austin 3 ton and more. He recently collected a 1932 Ford B van in excellent condition which had lain in a shed for many years .....

MALCOLM KEELEY, who took the photograph of this Merryweather (number 5593) and the Willys beyond it at Funchal, Madeira, says that there was once a fire museum on the island but that these and other exhibits are now housed with the modern appliances and plainly getting in the way .....

WE HEAR THAT Lancashire County Council is considering providing a building to be used as a national commercial vehicle museum. The location near so many past and present heavy vehicle manufacturers seems ideal and we await developments with interest .....

ON LOAN TO THE SCIENCE MUSEUM from Sunter Brothers and currently being restored by Edward Hannon in Shildon is one of only two Rotinoff Atlantic GR7s built in the late fifties for heavy haulage. It originally had a supercharged Rolls-Royce six cylinder 250 bhp diesel and eighteen speed Rotinoff gearbox but has been converted to R-R 300 bhp C type and SCG eight speed gearbox .....

THIS IS AN HISTORICALLY IMPORTANT vehicle languishing in a commercial vehicle breaker's yard between Coventry and Leicester. It is one of the eight wheel Scammell snow plough/gritter chassis developed when the M1 first opened. This example dates from 1960 and looked too good to break -- perhaps it will have a new lease of life as a heavy wrecker .....

SOME YEARS AGO we attended an auction near London Airport which contained a 1936 Garner six wheeler. The owner claimed to have only included it to get an idea of its value (£1000+) and we have often wondered what became of it. Now we have the answer. It was recently bought by P R Silverthorne of Maidenhead, who tells us that the Garner was originally owned by Riding Court Farm, Datchet, who used it for taking vegetables to the London market. Its Waukesha engine still runs well, the chrome is all greased over and the whole thing needs little more than a repaint. It set us delving in our archives where we came up with the view of it when new and awaiting delivery outside Garner's Acton works. Meanwhile, a very low mileage but completely rotten motor caravan based on a 1932 Garner is being offered for sale in Hampshire for £1000. Our other photograph shows the ex-Sparshatt and now Senior 1933 Garner as first discovered in Yorkshire in 1970 .....

AT MOUNT GAMBIER, South Africa, Mr G A Sturges is still using a 1909 Foden traction engine to run a chaff cutter. He supplies feed for racehorses and finds that piping steam through the hay cuts down dust and, therefore, respiratory difficulties amongst his customer's horses. He bought the engine in 1964 for $20 and says he wouldn't part with it, even though steam vehicles in his area have recently been fetching nearly $2500 apiece .....

IN SPAIN Charles Cawood tells us of two c1923 Aveling and Porter twin flywheel diesel rollers apparently still in use alongside the Malaga to Grenada road, about 20km from the former .....

ROBIN GAY has written from Australia to say that local enthusiasts have found the following vehicles and are anxious to obtain any information on them: four Albion LC24s with serial numbers 4032K, 4143F, 4245A and 4329C, a Republic model 19x25WC, Series 3, serial no 260599, and a Martini truck, approx 1909, and roughly 2 ton capacity, with disc wheels, solid rubber tyres, brass radiator and four cylinder Martini engine. He says that there is enough of the Albions to make up at least two very complete, original vehicles, and wonders what the letter after the serial number means. The Republic is very complete and original, but the Martini is missing many parts .....

WE SAW THIS AEC MERCURY tanker at a museum dispersal sale near Winchester in 1976 and as it only sold for about £175 we were afraid that it might be going for scrap. We now hear that is in good hands near Southampton and that it started life as an all-weather coach for Timpsons in 1930, chassis no 640069 (GN7317).

A GREAT WAR DORMAN 4JO 40hp Subsidy engine as used by various makes of three ton truck has come to light in Liphook. As its specification plate is in Russian, one can only assume that it was an export order frustrated by the Russian Revolution .....

MR ACLE on Medway 32979 has a number of *Commercial Motors* of the Second World War period that he would like to swap for earlier *CMs* or *Motor Transports*, preferably bound. We, too, would like to acquire similar magazines but are complete up to mid-1937. Let us know what you can spare - we could swap or buy

NICE TO KNOW that various local authorities in Scotland still use Second World War Mack 6x6 chassis to keep the snow at bay .....

THIS 1957 ALBION tractive unit is resting at the back of a works unit on the trading estate at Westbury, Wilts .....

A 1½ TON DODGE 6x6 of World War II onto which has been grafted an Austin cab. Nick Georgano saw the vehicle at a garage in Upton-on-Severn .....

EDDIE WAUGH writes from Sanquahar to say that the AEC Mercurys shown outside a transport café in our *KALEIDOSCOPE OF LORRIES & VANS* were on their way to Oswald Transport of Ayr from Boalloy when snapped. Oswald, apparently, is still very much in business and now owned by GKN. In the same book, G S C Rouse doubts that the factory we describe as belonging to Commer is, in fact, theirs, and he should know as he comes from Luton! So where is it, as this is definitely what was written on the back of the original photo?...

A GREAT RARITY TODAY, though once almost as popular as the O series Bedford was the Morris-Commercial Equi-load. This one was seen on a farm in Central Wales .....

JUDGING BY its registration number, this Atkinson, photographed (*right*) by M J Perry must date from 1953. The cab seems to be a proprietary type, perhaps by Duramin, and the vehicle is still in use in Somerset .....

THIS LITTLE COMMER of about 1938 was seen in a scrapyard near Shaftesbury .....

COLES CRANES celebrated their centenary in 1979 and 1982 will mark the sixtieth anniversary of their first Tilling-Stevens based lorry-mounted crane. We will hope to tell the full story in a future *ALBUM* and were interested to learn that Henry James Coles had worked for **Maudslay Sons and Field** before starting his own firm and moving from London to Derby in 1898, at the same time that Maudslays were heading for Coventry to become motor instead of ship engineers .....

THE OWNER OF THIS 1936 Leyland Beaver is Mr Tucker, 115 Bridgwater Rd, Bathpool, Taunton. He owns a scrapyard but decided that this 1936 Leyland Beaver ran so well when he collected it for scrap 20 years ago that he would keep it. He drove it into a neighbour's farmyard and there it rests to this day, half smothered in brambles. He would now be glad to sell it .....

ON SHOW IN THE MUSEUM attached to the Royal Family's Norfolk retreat, Sandringham House, are a number of Daimler shooting brakes going back to before the Great War and a 1937 Morris-Commercial Ajax fire appliance. A beam engine that had once generated electricity on the estate has recently been donated to the Ironbridge Gorge Museum .....

REFERENCE TO THE PIONEER British Kerr-Stuart diesel lorry in our companion volume *KALEIDOSCOPE OF LORRIES AND VANS* has prompted a reader to enquire how many were built. Unfortunately, we do not know the answer, but one shown in *Motor Transport* recently went to R Howle, Chesterton, Stoke-on-Trent, and Chris Taylor has been investigating another which appeared in the late Charles Klapper's *Old Lorries* book. It was TX 8955, registered in February 1930 as a tipper for use by F W Lougher at Pontalun Quarry near Bridgend. It only remained there until June when it disappeared until 1934. It then emerged in the registration records with a smaller 120mm bore (135mm before) engine in the hands of the North British Locomotive Co. It was last registered to April 1937. Do any railway enthusiasts know if loco maker Kerr-

Stuart was involved with North British? If so it will mean that Kerr-Stuart and Halley were linked at the time as Halley was 50% owned by North British between 1930 and the end in 1935

THIS WARTIME CANADIAN FORD truck is languishing beside a garage in the one-time railway village of Melton Constable in Norfolk. It has been used as a breakdown truck for many years but now appears to be out of use .....

AN UNUSUAL SIGHT IN BRITAIN is this air-cooled six cylinder Praga V35 6x6 three tonner currently undergoing restoration by the Imperial War Museum. It dates from the mid-fifties .....

THE LONG SHOP at the Garrett works at Leiston in Suffolk is to be preserved and will house a selection of products made by this famous firm and also its associates in the onetime Agricultural and General Engineers combine, which included several commercial vehicle makers. It would be nice to see Jack Butler's Garrett wagon alongside Nick Baldwin's Caledon (a firm run by Garrett in its final year) .....

THIS IS AN OLD FRIEND of OLD MOTOR which is plainly still in use at Neujport near Ostend as Tim Nicholson has taken another picture of it. We still think that it is a Saurer, but can anyone identify it positively? .....

DAVID AKEHURST, Fairview Garage, Fairview Avenue, Gillingham, Kent, has rescued a 1920 Albion A20 that was used for many years as works transport by a carpet firm in Barnsley. To assist in its rebuild he needs a worm back axle, radiator and suitable headlights .....

WARSTONE'S preserved O series Bedford beside one of their TKs. A pity about the anachronistic registration number .....

WE NEVER FAIL to be amazed at the way obscure makes of vehicle continue to turn up. The latest is a 1931 Beardmore Cobra ten ton road tractor which had belonged to Watney's Mortlake Brewery when new and had been sent to its maltings at Tivetshall in East Anglia sometime after the war. Apparently, the last of Watney's six or so Beardmores in London was scrapped as recently as 1966 so the survivor was plainly lucky to have been equipped with wooden buffers and pensioned off as a yard and railway siding shunter at Tivetshall. It is believed to have been out of use for some fifteen years and last Christmas was rescued by G Boden of Hethersett, who plans to restore it. Its 50 bhp four cylinder Meadows petrol engine started without difficulty and all its five forward gears seem to work. Its enormous rear axle was assumed to be a two-speeder but contemporary literature suggests that it was a double reduction unit with differential lock controlled by a pedal in the cab. This and a weight transferring screw acting on the drawbar of the two axle trailer that it normally hauled must have given it almost as good traction as the contemporary 4x4 Latil.

The survival of this Beardmore is made all the more extraordinary by the fact that these road tractors only existed for two years (1930-32) under this name (Beardmore took up the licence in December 1929 but did not make any until late in 1930). They were previously French Chenard et Walckers, built under licence by Hall, Lewis & Co, and afterwards were known as Multi-wheelers, being produced in London by the trailer firm of this name for a few years. However, very few under any of these names can have entered service, though in 1930 Chenards spoke of 1000 having been produced in France since 1920.....

WE WERE SAD TO HEAR of the recent death of Gordon Mackenzie Junner, the editor of *Commercial Motor* from 1929 to 1959. He was 88 and had joined *CM* from AEC in 1913. After war service, he returned to *CM*, where he handled technical matters and became an expert on diesel development. He was founder of the forerunner of the Road Haulage Association, which was created to improve the tarnished image of road haulage in the twenties. He was also responsible for the later Institute of Road Transport Engineers. He had a great spirit of fun and enjoyed practical jokes, much to the consternation of his staff and, with his familiar goatee beard, he was a familiar figure at Commercial Motor Shows until they left London .....

STILL ON THE SUBJECT of Morris-Commercials, here we have an early fifties van seen by M J Perry at Phillips Coaches, Holywell, Flint .....

WHEN LOOKING AT THE HISTORY of Douglas special vehicles in *No 1*, we wondered how many of their trucks were still around. One occasionally sees the Matador-based logging type, but on a recent trip on the A1 near Huntingdon we came across a 1960 timber truck looking very much like the four wheel steering example we showed, but with only front axle steering. It was standing battered in a field but appeared to be still in use .....

This grand old lady of haulage, a 1931 Leyland Hippo, was one of many 6 wheelers which had second steering axles added later. In this case the new axle came off an AEC. The operators, Wm Bowker of Blackburn, Lancs, had one of the finest 8 wheeler fleets in the UK. Makes included Leyland, Atkinson, ERF and Guy.

RIGID EIGHT WHEELERS

For three decades the rigid eight was the flagship of British truck haulage fleets until it was knocked from favour by the big artics. PETER J DAVIES has always admired these curiously British machines and looks at the history of their development, their recent return to popularity, and the growing Continental interest in them since the sixties.

RIGID 8 wheelers have been built by over fifty manufacturers in fifteen different countries. In spite of this, they are still widely thought of as a British speciality. Rightly so, for it was in the UK that the rigid eight caught on in a big way during the forties and fifties.

Quite an important landmark in British transport legislation was the passing of the 1930 Road Traffic Act which, among other things,

laid down size and weight limits for heavy trucks. Prior to this Act, goods vehicles had been developed within a much looser framework of legislation, influenced considerably by military requirements. To some extent the sizes and weights of vehicles had been limited by available engine power, strength of materials and by the strength of the road surfaces over which they operated. Very early vehicle develop-

ment in the UK was hampered by the 'Red Flag Act' (1865-1896) and many important 'firsts' fell to countries other than Britain, notably Germany, France and America. History shows that the earliest experiments with 'multi-axle rigids' took place in the USA. It is interesting, and perhaps a little ironical, that North America pioneered the early rigids and later became the home of the articulated vehicle,

JANVIER TWIN-STEER, 1906

whilst the UK can lay claim to the first artic (1897 Thornycroft steamer) but later became the home of the rigid eight wheeler.

In 1918/19 while UK manufacturers were concentrating on solid tyred four wheelers for maximum payloads of around 4 tons, the Goodyear Tyre & Rubber Co in Ohio were experimenting with six wheeled trucks and buses to help promote the use of larger pneumatic truck tyres on heavy vehicles. Hitherto, pneumatics originating in the 1850s had been confined to motor cars and light commercials, heavier vehicles being equipped with solids. One of the Goodyear experimental vehicles was reputedly a 'double bogie' rigid eight wheeled bus, the body of which was adapted from a single deck tramcar. Another interesting American vehicle, although not a commercial, was the Reeves 'Octo-Auto' 8 wheeled passenger car of 1911. The Reeves company was also Ohio based and the Octo-Auto's highly revolutionary concept may have influenced the early designs of two axle bogies on trucks. One or two other American manufacturers came up with rigid eights although these were all slightly unconventional concepts which came and went in the 1920s.

REEVES 'OCTO-AUTO', 1911

Going back even further, a French vehicle designer in or around 1906 built what must surely have been the earliest six wheeled rigid commercial. The Janvier chassis had a unique two axle front bogie. This layout was to reappear in the UK in the 1930s and became popularly known as the 'Chinese Six'. One important feature common to the Janvier and to the Reeves car was the 'rocking beam' arrangement of the suspension which reduced the vertical travel of the chassis when the wheels travelled over a bump.

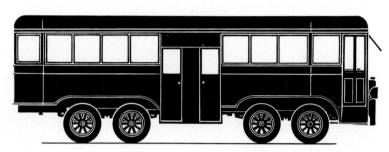

GOODYEAR BUS, 1919

This ability of vehicles with two spring tandem axle bogies to 'hug the ground' led to its eventual adoption in light military vehicles during the mid-1920s, partly as a means of improving ride and traction in off-road conditions. Rigid six wheeled truck and passenger vehicles evolved rapidly during the latter half of the 1920s. The UK's popular heavy four wheeled steam wagons were able to carry greater payloads with the addition of the third axle. Manufacturers like Sentinel, Foden, Garrett and Yorkshire all turned out a 'rigid six' suitable for payloads of around 12 tons. Petrol engined six wheelers were also appearing on the UK scene from manufacturers like Leyland, Maudslay and Scammell. Atkinsons in Preston, Lancashire, among other firms, carried out third axle conversions on various makes during the period before production of Atkinson diesel vehicles had begun. Where the majority of countries stuck to the six wheeler as the 'maximum capacity' haulage vehicle, the UK went a step further with the introduction of the first rigid 8 wheeler. This came late in 1929 when Sentinel built what was basically a DG6 wagon with a new 4 wheel steering front bogie.

The new vehicle, called the DG8, had a gross weight of 23 tons and a payload of 14/15 tons

PHILLIPSON'S QUARRY
COX GREEN.
NR. BOLTON
TELEPHONE:-
37.
EAGLEY.
No 3
P.J.DAVIES '71

Sentinel really started it all with this solid tyred steam driven giant in 1930. Sadly, its high unladen weight was to inhibit its sales until the S8 appeared in the mid-thirties.

How the front bogie of the Sentinel DG8 steered. Note the unusual trunnion arrangement round which the wheels on each side pivoted.

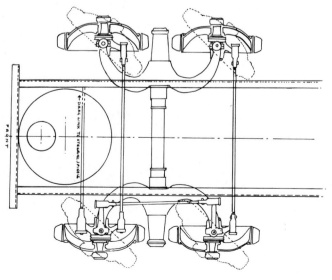

One of the most innovative rigid eights was the Scammell in 1937 which had a very low unladen weight thanks to rubber rear suspension, 8x2 and load equalising front suspension. It was little changed over 20 years and a 1946 example is shown.

The 1939 Miesse rigid 8 wheeler built in Belgium had a wide spaced rear bogie with single tyred self-steering trailing fourth axle. A unique feature was the roof mounted radiator.

While British manufacturers in the late thirties were well into rigid 8s, other European countries stayed with the 6 wheeler. One German manufacturer, however, Faun, developed this L1500 D87 model [1938 example shown] with Humboldt Deutz diesel engine. It was designed to carry 15 tons and to British eyes it had very unusual lines.

In the USA rigid 8 wheelers were uncommon. The Spangler Dual of 1947/9 was a particularly curious looking machine with twin wheels on all axles and twin Ford V8 petrol engines each driving a separate rear axle.

was possible. So the 8 wheeler had appeared - derived from the 6 wheeler and signifying another important step forward in the search for more efficient bulk transport of goods.

Coinciding with the appearance of the Sentinel DG8 in 1929/30 came the new Road Traffic Act laying down specific limits for weights and dimensions of road vehicles. These remained in force substantially unchanged for 20 years. Broadly speaking, the limits were: 12 tons for 2 axles, 19 tons for 3 axles (16 tons if of the twin steering layout) and 22 tons for vehicles 'with more than 3 axles'. For steam lorries with pneumatic tyres weights were slightly higher at 14 and 20 tons for four and six wheelers respectively.

Average payloads on the 2 axled and 3 axled vehicles were 8 and 12 tons respectively. With its additional front steering axle, the 8 wheeler's average payload was 14 to 15 tons. The early 8 wheelers were, in the majority of cases, simply based on 6 wheelers with a second steering axle added. Power units, transmissions and axles were identical. So, for the penalty of another ton or so on the unladen weight, the 8 wheeler could carry roughly 2 extra tons payload. It made economic sense for haulage operators to put 8 wheelers to work, particularly where maximum payloads were required to be moved over long distances. In fact, some practically minded operators carried out conversions on 6 wheelers to win the extra load capacity. It is believed that a haulier in Yorkshire pre-empted the first British-built internal combustion engined roadgoing 8 wheeler by converting an AEC 6 wheeler in 1933. Certainly some of the early rigid eights which appear in photographs of the period were not production models.

The Associated Equipment Company of Southall, Middlesex, was the first manufacturer to introduce an internal combustion engined 8 wheeler. This was the famous Mammoth Major, announced in February 1934. Close on AEC's heels came Armstrong-Saurer of Newcastle-on-Tyne with their 'Samson', which remained in production for only four years. The Mammoth Major marque, by contrast, was to remain with us for many years and was probably one of the best known rigid eights of all.

This general arrangement drawing of a 1934 Armstrong Saurer Samson clearly shows the forward thinking of the designers. The Samson was very advanced, having all the characteristics of the more sophisticated post-war 8 wheelers. Its parallel channel side members and simple four spring rear suspension pre-empted later developments by other manufacturers. It even had a spiral bevel rear axle, full air operated braking on all 8 wheels with manual pressure setting to minimise wheel lock-up when running unladen.

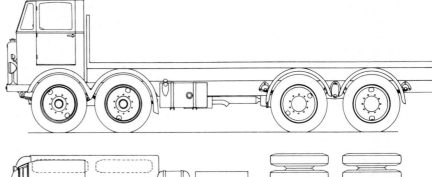

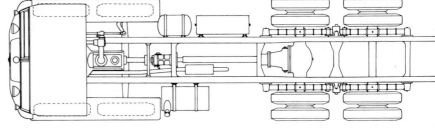

Rigid eights held considerable military attractions when 8x8 because of their extra off-road traction. One of the first was this Guy with 96 bhp petrol engine in 1931, followed soon afterwards by examples from Leyland and AEC.

In the closing weeks of 1939 Maudslay began building 8 wheelers at their Parkside, Coventry, factory. They were called Mikados. Only nine were built. Later, certain firms added second steers to Maharajah 6 wheelers. This is one such vehicle. There were numerous others virtually indistinguishable from their Mikado big sisters.

Sentinel built only a small number of DG8s before the introduction of their more advanced S8 model in 1934.

Thus the British 8 wheeler era dawned. Nearly every other heavy lorry manufacturer in the UK followed AEC and Armstrong-Saurer as the demand for 'rigid eights' grew, and by the close of the 1930s there were no less than eight makes on the market, not counting Yorkshire and Armstrong-Saurer, which had already ceased production.

ERF Limited, formed at Sandbach, Cheshire, in 1933 had rapidly graduated from their first 6/8 ton four wheeler to a full range of heavy trucks, including a maximum gross rigid eight (the C16.8) by the end of 1934. Nearby at Fodens' works, the S type 8 wheeler was taking shape to make its debut in 1935. Scammell Lorries in Watford, famous for their articulated 8 wheelers, brought out their rigid eight in 1936 which embodied some unique features, particularly in the suspension system. It is worth noting that Scammell's use of the type designation 'Rigid Eight' in order to distinguish the vehicle from the established Scammell 'Eight Wheeler' artic probably helped to consolidate this universal term into the language. Also to appear early that year was the Leyland Octopus, first of a famous line and now the longest surviving marque out of the many 8 wheeler manufacturers who were absorbed into the Leyland group in the fifties. 1936 saw the introduction of the Yorkshire WK6, a bid by the famous steam wagon manufacturers from Hunslet, Leeds, to capture their share of the diesel engined rigid eight market. Albion Motors of Scotstoun, Glasgow, were also into the heavyweight rigid business in 1936 with their T561 8 wheeler, a somewhat rarer machine than the more familiar CX7 model which came on the scene in 1938. Before the close of the thirties two more well-known makes of rigid eight were launched - Atkinson Lorries (1933) Ltd of Preston brought out their L1486 model in 1937; the Maudslay Motor Company in Coventry built their first Mikado 8 wheeler in the closing months of 1939. Further development on the 8 wheeler front generally was curtailed by the strengthening grip of wartime austerity. Only nine Mikados were built in total, the last being completed in July 1941.

Britain was by no means the sole exponent of the rigid eight in the 1930s but it is safe to say that this special breed of truck never proliferated elsewhere as it did in the UK. Certain Continental manufacturers, notably Miesse in Brussels and Faun-Werke GmbH in Nurem-

Atkinson was another early firm to develop a successful eight wheeler and it was one of the few to be given a permit to produce them for essential transport services in the Second World War.

The 1935 Straussler was something of a curiosity among 8 wheelers. This view shows the sharply cambered wheels, due to all-round independent suspension, and 'bug like' frontal appearance. It was powered by a 150 bhp V8 petrol engine driving the two sets of front wheels.

berg, designed and built rigid eights in the late
thirties. The payload capacity of these was not
too different from the British models at 15/16
tons, but to British eyes they were both somewhat alien with wheelbases and front and rear
overhangs quite different from the stereotyped
22 ton gross machines in the UK. The rigid
4 axle configuration was also being applied to
military vehicles prior to and during World
War II. Here, of course, the need was for
traction and mobility in off-road situations.
Certain American manufacturers, including
Sterling Corbitt Cook, Ford and GMC, built
such '8x8' machines as did the Swiss firm of
Adolph Saurer at Arbon. Similarly, France,
Russia and Poland produced 8 wheeled military
vehicles. Great Britain was no exception, with
8x8s coming from Thornycroft (the Terrapin)
and Albion. Other experimental 8x8s had
appeared even earlier in the 1930s from Morris-

**Thirty years ago this Foden FG6/15 was
representative of the largest haulage vehicles in
the UK. This machine was one of a huge fleet
run by British Road Services and was photographed on the day of delivery to W T Parrott of
Luton in February 1949.**

**Much of the appeal of lorries and trucks lies in
their pleasing appearance. Even before its
handsome Jennings streamlined cab was fitted,
this 1951 ERF 6.8 could not fail to kindle
enthusiasm. In this picture is perhaps the
ultimate blend of the finest components and
expertise. As with any great engineering work,
this machine radiates visual harmony.**

**The PF NR6 Trusty [1946-56] was the 8 wheeler
offered by the famous pioneer truck builder
John I Thornycroft of Basingstoke, Hampshire.
It had 8 wheel air brakes as standard. The one
shown is typical of the maximum capacity trunk
vehicles which ran between Yorkshire and
London during the fifties.**

The KCP owned AEC Mammoth Major is an early example from 1934, the year in which AEC introduced the world's first diesel engined production eight wheeler for general road haulage.

A 1953 Mk III Mammoth Major, one of approximately 1700 of this type giving yeoman service in the UK and overseas.

The Mk V Mammoth Major was introduced in 1958 with 11.3 litre diesel and six speed gearbox. This is one of the last before the Leyland Ergomatic tilt cab was adopted and dates from 1965.

Commercial, Armstrong-Siddeley and Guy. The Guy of 1931 was unusual in being normal control (see *KALEIDOSCOPE OF LORRIES & VANS*) and it was soon followed by other 8x8 off-road lorries from Leyland and AEC in 1932/3 (see *VINTAGE LORRY ANNUAL NO 1*).

One interesting British 8x4 front wheel drive vehicle which fell somewhere between the conventional civilian 8 wheeler and the more specialised all wheel drive military 8 wheeler was the unique Straussler. This vehicle, announced in October 1936, was a curious blend of innovative engineering features quite different from any other British rigid 8 wheeler so far produced. Although British in origin, the Straussler 8x4 was, in fact, built in Hungary for the engineer Nicholas Straussler, whose UK factory was at Brentford in Middlesex. Only one example of the 8x4 was produced, this being to the special requirements of the Anglo Iranian Oil Company. the normal type of rigid 8 simply was not suited to the severe conditions encountered transporting bulk petroleum (gasolene) from the Persian Gulf to Teheran. A higher degree of mobility and stability was required. This was achieved by the Straussler with its all-round independent suspension, extra

The only make of rigid 8 wheeler ever to come from 'North of the Border' was the Scotstoun-built Albion. This 1938 CX7N model is an example of the best known type. Superbly turned out, as only the Scots know how, in the traditional green, red and tartan finery of McCall and Greenshields, Kilmarnock.

British Road Services fleet at the height of the nationalisation era in 1952-53 had some 3½ thousand rigid 8 wheelers, none more character-istic than this Leyland 22.01 Octopus. The South Wales steel towns were served by fleets of rigid 8 flats, dropsides and coilers. Between the Bridgend, Swansea, Cardiff and Newport depôts alone there were nearly 300. This one is shown waiting to offload its cargo of sheet steel at a large motor factory in the early sixties.

low centre of gravity, front wheel drive and powerful V8 petrol engine. The weight distribution was split more or less evenly on the front and rear bogies and the heavy duty Goodyear 12.75 x 20 balloon tyres each carried approximately 3 tons when fully laden. Individual steering boxes served each front wheel and the turning circle of 60ft was good but not exceptional for a vehicle measuring 25ft 10ins long by 8ft wide. The Straussler V8 petrol engine had a bore and stroke of 98mm x 120mm, giving a swept volume of 7200cc. At 2800 rpm it developed an impressive 150 bhp. In top gear on the 6 speed synchromesh transmission the Straussler could keep up 40 mph, fast for a heavy vehicle in the mid-1930s. Fuel consumption, not a serious matter in view of the operator's trade, was in the region of 5 mpg so the 200 gallon fuel tank incorporated into the main 3700 gallon Thompson Bros tank body provided an impressive range of 1000 miles.

Whilst these various civilian and military vehicles all come under the common heading Eight Wheelers, the two divide into quite separate groups. Few, if any, of the military eights were based on civilian haulage vehicles; ordinary civilian rigid eights have, of course, been operated widely by the British Armed Forces during and since World War II.

The peculiarly British species of rigid 8x2 and 8x4 vehicles which followed on from the early DG8s and Mammoth Majors adhered to the same basic layout and overall proportions for upwards of thirty years and even today's rigid 8s, though heavier, longer and wider, are still not strikingly different. The biggest advances in recent years have been the adoption of 8 wheeled braking, tilt cabs and, more recently still, sleeper cabs. Rigid 8s were once the largest and most impressive vehicles in British haulage fleets, but since new legislation in 1964 they have been progressively relegated to more specialised rôles as bulk tippers and tankers. Looking back to the immediate post-World War II period when European vehicles in the UK were few and far between, the list of British 8 wheeler manufacturers was impressive and many new models were appearing on the market during the late forties and early fifties. The late forties was a difficult time for the vehicle industry with raw material shortages and restrictions on sales to the home market. The pressure was on to build up the export trade well beyond the pre-war level. The mandate was

Before legislative changes took place in 1964 rigid eights grossed 24 tons but could legally haul a four wheel independent drawbar trailer at a permitted 32 tons. This 1959 Seddon DD8 with trailer was an unusual sight as most DD8s were designed as solo machines. Some had a design weight of 28 tons when the UK limit was only 24. This vehicle, photographed during a stop en route from Sittingbourne to Barrow-in-Furness, is loaded with paper goods.

given to commercial vehicle manufacturers to export 60% of their production. The famine of new vehicles in the UK during and after the war created a strong demand, but manufacturers, due to steel shortages and their commitments to export markets, were finding it difficult to fulfil home demand. In this period British manufacturers found themselves designing or adapting models which would suit the home market and also appeal to the many countries throughout the British Commonwealth. Export requirements eventually influenced the design of

Sentinel have the distinction of being the first manufacturers to have built a rigid 8 wheeled haulage lorry. Oddly, Sentinel were about the only British manufacturer not to market an oil engined rigid 8, their only two offerings, the DG8 and S8, being steam powered. The underslung engine on the Sentinel DV6/6 oiler precluded the addition of a second steer. When Sentinels ceased production in 1957, a consortium of hauliers in the north west of England got together with the Sentinel main dealer, North Cheshire Motors of Warrington, and built these rigid 8s, using Sentinel chassis parts but powered by a vertical front mounted oil engine. They called them TVWs. Several were built, powered by a variety of engine types.

A common sight in the fifties and sixties was this type of outfit for carrying long beams, girders or pipes. Often the rigid 8 was fitted with a normal platform with an inset mounting plate for the front bolster. The dolly was secured to the rear of the load and brake pipes and electrical connections strung along the underside. This particular Scammell-hauled outfit is, in effect, an articulated vehicle. The majority of these outfits, many of which were operated by British Road Services, have now given way to normal tractor units, sometimes with extending trailers.

Not an example of the 28 ton Dodge-Unipower SEO rigid 8s launched in 1972 but a Primrose conversion carried out some three years earlier on a Perkins V8 powered KT900. This ultra short machine grossed at 24 tons. Primrose Third Axle Co Ltd of Blackburn in Lancashire carried out numerous such conversions throughout the 1960s and 1970s giving rise to some fascinating 'one-offs' based on a wide range of makes like Bedford, BMC and Ford.

vehicles - rigid 8s included - which, in some cases, were given more powerful engines, extra cooling capacity and heavier duty tyres.

Left hand steering options became more generally available. British 8 wheeeled rigids were exported to South Africa, Australia, South America and many other countries. The export drive reached out to Scandinavia, the Netherlands, Belgium, Greece, India, Ceylon, Iran and beyond. By 1950 Great Britain was the world's largest exporter of commercial vehicles, with Australia, New Zealand and South Africa among its biggest customers. Rigid 8s admittedly formed only a small percentage of the total but, nevertheless, operators in many countries had the opportunity to see and try these singularly British 'monsters'. In one country in particular - Australia - they have remained a popular type of vehicle and 8 wheelers are in wide use there currently, many of them being Australian designed and built, like the International, Leader and RFW. Japanese makes including Isuzu also figure in the current 8 wheeler scene in Australia.

Few other countries produced rigid eights in the post-war years. A handful of somewhat unconventional types appeared from US manufacturers, often for special purpose transport. Perhaps the strangest was the Spangler Dual, named thus because of its dual Ford V8 power units. Ford mechanical units were used throughout. It also had dual front tyres as well as dual rears. The front and rear bogies with coil suspension took an equal share of the fully laden truck's 20 tons. The front wheels were steered by dual ratio steering, the lower ratio, which was selected by a steering column mounted lever, being for manoeuvring at low speeds. The Dual was shod on sixteen 7.50 x 20 tyres on 5 stud wheels. Twenty-seven feet of body space was available within the 33ft overall length. The top speed was claimed to be nearly 70 mph - not bad with 14 tons up! A very attractive and ingenious vehicle.

But the UK reigned throughout the fifties and sixties as the 8 wheeler centre of the world. This period is thought of as the heyday of the rigid eight in British haulage. There is no doubt that, during the 20 years from 1945 to 1965, British operators and drivers held the rigid 8 in high esteem, since they were the biggest and best trucks on the road. Vehicles like the Leyland Octopus, the AEC Mammoth Major, the Foden FG 6/15 and the Atkinson L1586 travelled every major trunk route in the country. There were 14 makes in all, including such illustrious names as Thornycroft, ERF, Guy, Seddon, Maudslay, Albion, Scammell and Bristol. Until new vehicles became more freely available in the late forties, there were many examples of pre-war rigid eights still running, including Yorkshires and Armstrong-Saurers. These were not to last much beyond the mid-fifties and the motorway era was not far away. Faster, more powerful 'wheelers', as they are sometimes affectionately known, were required to cope with the kind of high pressure operation which has grown up since the advent of the motorways in the late fifties.

To compare the British 8 wheeler of the 1935 to 1955 period with that which emerged in the late 1950s is interesting. The typical rigid eight from the earlier period would have an 8 litre 110 bhp diesel engine (petrol engines were also available in the thirties), 4 speed gearbox and auxiliary or booster box, overhead worm drive axles, a gross weight of 22 tons, a 24ft body (7ft 5ins wide), 6 wheel brakes, usually hydraulic, ratchet multi-pull handbrake, 40 gallon fuel tank, manual steering with 21ins diameter 4 spoke wheel, cast aluminium radiator with replaceable tubes, separate opening windscreens, one single electric wiper with a 10ins blade and a somewhat noisy and

Drivers and crews on brewery trucks need a low platform. Small wheels on two axle trucks limit your gross weight and your braking performance. One solution to the problem was to increase the number of wheels. On the one hand these Leyland Lairds with Primrose second and fourth axle conversions carried the payload, kept the platform low and increased brake frictional area; on the other hand, they had drawbacks in tyre wear and steering alignment.

Isuzu trucks were marketed in Australia under the Bedford name. This impressive rigid 8 wheeled 'Bedford' is a conversion built by Bartlett Trailers Pty Ltd of Clayton, Victoria. In response to demand, Isuzu have since launched their own factory-built SPH710 in 1978. They have a gross weight of 28 tons and are powered by a turbocharged Isuzu E120 12 litre straight six diesel. Transmission is the Fuller RT 9509A.

draughty steel panelled wood framed cab. Heaters were accessories for those who wanted them. By the late fifties the gross weight had risen to 24 tons and 32 tons was permitted with a drawbar trailer equipped with power brakes.

(In fact, the initial 1930 legislation which restricted trailers to 4 wheelers was amended late in 1942 to allow trailers behind 6 and 8 wheelers.) Braking, by then mostly air, was still on three axles on the majority of makes, but 8 wheeled braking was optional on a few. Some drivers argued that on slippery roads the unbraked front wheels of the earlier vehicles were a boon as they helped to maintain adhesion when braking. More powerful engines up to 150 bhp with 6 speed overdrive transmissions were coming in but many manufacturers still employed worm drive rear axles which were not ideally suited to high speed operation. Top speeds had risen from around 35 mph to approximately 55 mph. Probably the biggest area of improvement was the cab, where large wrap-round windshields had become the vogue and heaters were standard fitting. Power assisted steering was still uncommon and the driver's environment was still rather spartan compared with vehicles of the late seventies. Times of great change were just around the corner in the shape of the Road Traffic Act of 1964.

The 1964 Act set out to bring UK vehicles more into line with Europe and the rest of the

The Spanish have a very singular style of rigid 8 as exemplified by this Pegaso for 35 tonnes gvw. For running unladen some have hydraulic lift on the second and fourth axles. This early sixties 1066 32 ton gross tanker seen in Santurce, near Bilbao, has the second pair of wheels raised. The rearmost axle, as with the majority of Spanish 8 wheelers, is of the single tyred, trailing, self-steering type.

Australia is probably second only to Britain as a nation of rigid 8s. This 1978 International Harvester ACCO [Type AAA] is a good example of the purpose-built rigids developed specially for the Australian market and built at the Dandenong plant of IH Australia Ltd. Other Australian makes include Leader and RFW.

world. Increasing international traffic demanded that something be done. The Europeanisation of British haulage began and the thirty year reign of the rigid eight was more or less at an end. An intriguing attempt to bestow a continuing rôle upon the doomed 24 ton rigid was made by Fodens Ltd when they surprised artic-hungry Britain with their unique 32 ton Twin Load. This was a load-carrying

rigid eight tractor unit with a factory built single axle semi trailer. This could, perhaps, be called a 'dromedary' style outfit. It did not catch on in a big way. There was a rapid growth in production of tractor units for 32 ton gross weight and, of course, in the production of maximum capacity semi trailers. A few specialist firms, some of whom had trailer manufacturing interests, made a practice of converting the now 'redundant' rigid eights into tractor units and a lot of familiar eight-leggers of large fleets reappeared in a new rôle to join the purpose-built tractors in the swing to articulation. The sales of rigid eights plummeted during the late 1960s.

But eight-leggers continued to be offered by the best known manufacturers like Foden, ERF, Atkinson and the Leyland Group, which included AEC, Guy and Scammell. These were employed largely on bulk tipper work or on 'domestic' operations where the 8 wheeler was still superior - tanker work, brick haulage, and so on. Tilt cabs became more common, as did the use of glass reinforced plastics. Eight wheel air brakes, power steering and spiral bevel axles were the norm. The 1964 Act, while opening the door to articulation and, incidentally, the

approaching flood of European heavy tractor units, also granted the rigid eight a somewhat insignificant increase in weight and size. The product of this legislative manoeuvre was a somewhat unwieldy beast, so long in the wheelbase that sharp corners and narrow junctions presented real problems!

In order for the 8 wheeler manufacturers to take advantage of the extra 4 tons, bringing the gross weight to the new permitted maximum of 28, the outer axle spread had to be 26 feet (8m). This resulted in turning circles in excess of 100ft (31m). Lock angles were improved on one hand by the new 8ft 2½in (2½m) overall width, but this was negated by having larger tyres.

Further legislation came in 1972 which eased this situation by shortening the minimum axle spreads for higher gross weights. What emerged from this somewhat messy legislation was a new and better integrated breed of rigid eight, capable of operating at 30 tons gvw. At the 1970 Earl's Court Exhibition, Guy Motors boldly announced a new 350 bhp 30 ton rigid Big J8, having gone for a period without an 8 wheeler. The new model optimistically assumed a legal 56 tons train weight limit on British roads. In the event the GTW stayed at 32 tons. The outcome was the demise of the 8 wheeler and trailer outfit.

Sales of 30 ton rigids began to rise as operators discovered that articulation was for certain types of traffic not the 'be all and end all' that it was first thought to be. During the past eight years or so, rigid eights have not only climbed back up the sales graph to treble in numbers, but their importance was recognised by the same major European truck builders as leaped into the tractor unit market in the mid-sixties. Volvo, DAF, Magirus Deutz and MAN were quick to see the potential in building 30 ton 8 wheelers. British manufacturers, in their efforts to go articulated, had overlooked the 8 wheeler revival and now European eight-leggers are rubbing shoulders with such revered makes as Scammell, Leyland, ERF and Foden. The seventies not only saw a revival of the British rigid eight, but also striking changes in Europe. Swiss regulations in 1972 brought about a dramatic increase in British style 8 wheelers. Suddenly there were makes never witnessed before on the European scene. Although the roads of Italy had, since the early sixties, been crammed with rigid eights from OM and Fiat (often converted by OMT, who themselves built a few AEC engined 8 wheelers), such vehicles had not caught on elsewhere. Spain have their own rigid eights in the form of 35 ton Pegasos and Barreiros (now called Dodge).

Amongst the offerings on the Swiss market are some very impressive vehicles indeed for 28 tons gross operation. In general proportions they echo the classic formula of the British eights in their heyday. The makes include FBW, Saurer, Berna and a few from Mowag. With the now familiar names of Volvo, Scania, DAF, MAN, Steyr and Magirus Deutz, they are all in on the 8 wheeler boom. The European trend to rigid eight has also spread to Holland and Germany. In Holland, FTF make rigid eights and Terberg and Ginaf cater for heavy civil engineering work with specialist 8 wheel rigids. The most recent addition to the ranks is the Mercedes.

With this extraordinary revival of the rigid eight, this one-time oddity of the British Isles has taken on a new status. More are finding their way back into normal day-to-day long distance haulage. Cab interiors now have much improved levels of comfort and many operators are buying rigids with sleeper cabs. In spite of legislation, and the sometimes muddled interpretation of new regulations, it looks as if the rigid eight has carved a niche for itself in the truck scene of the 1980s.

FINDING A JEFFERY QUAD

**Years ago we saw a Jeffery Quad in France and took a keen interest
in its recovery. This is the story of how it recently came to England
and of the background to the unusual features of this important model.**

ON a visit to the Le Mans 24 Hours
Race in 1970, Nick Baldwin called at
the car museum on the circuit and was
surprised to see a 1914-18 American
army truck mouldering in a field
beyond the car park. The truck was a
Jeffery Quad, so named because of its
unusual four wheel drive and four
wheel steering. Enquiries at the
museum suggested that the Jeffery
had been a circuit maintenance truck
and would one day become an exhibit,

which seemed unlikely as it would
have been the only non-French one on
display in what was anyway a car
museum.

A photograph of the Jeffery
subsequently appeared in *OLD
MOTOR MAGAZINE* and was
spotted there by Richard Peskett, who
filed it away and thought no more of it
until last year, when he had finished
his well-known 1919 Fiat and was
looking for a fresh challenge. He

asked us about the Quad's where-
abouts and whether it was still there.
We did not know what had become of
it and could only give very vague
directions, but it was enough to
persuade Richard to take a chance
and he and friends Ivor Thompson
and Tony Cornish booked a cross
channel ferry and set out in a Ford

**Richard Peskett and Ivor Thompson take a
moment's break from clearing the undergrowth.**

platform truck. Enquiries in the neighbourhood resulted in blank stares and they had shown the *OLD MOTOR* photograph to some fifteen people and were feeling thoroughly despondent before a farmer said, 'Oh yes, I remember it being driven here in 1947, it's over there'.

They followed the line of his outstretched arm and could see nothing except a thicket, but sure enough the Quad was in it, in complete contrast to the wide open spaces surrounding it when we had first taken our photographs. Time and a fire had taken its toll of the woodwork and various bits had been removed from its Buda engine, including the carburettor, magneto and water inlet casting. Also missing was the coil spring mounted radiator. However, various small pieces were rescued from the mud and ash under the chassis and the whole thing was in far better condition than if it had stood in a damp British wood or scrapyard.

After hacking down the undergrowth, the Quad was pulled out with a block and tackle to the accompaniment of incredulous comments from some locals which, loosely translated, would come out as 'ah, zeez foolish Engleez, zey all 'ave zee screw loose'! Lest it sound as though Richard Peskett and friends were helping themselves to the Quad, it should be pointed out that they had, by now, bought it from the museum's patrons, The Auto Club de l'Oeust, who had generously charged a modest 3000 francs because they were pleased to see it going to a good home. The Customs took a similarly magnanimous view and did not charge duty on such a 'wreck'.

The Autojumble at Beaulieu produced an Eisemann G4 magneto and a carburettor and the Ford Museum at Dearborn, which had been contacted about Nash and Jeffery material, really came up trumps and not only supplied an original handbook and literature but, for $20, a radiator badge as well. An American owner of a Duplex truck volunteered a Pierce governor, so little by little all the missing parts were replaced.

The chassis has now been completely dismantled and, by the time this article appears, its restoration should be well underway. Curiously enough, despite its popularity in the Great War (it outnumbered the broadly similar but two wheel steered FWD, which has survived in reasonable numbers) none are known in Britain apart from a chassis at Leighton Buzzard, and a Nash version

How the Quad looked when seen at the Le Mans car park in 1970.

Richard Peskett and Ivor Thompson share an aperitif with the French farmer who remembered the Quad arriving in 1947.

imported by Tony Oliver on the very same day that the Jeffery disembarked at Southampton.

As already mentioned, the Quad's chief claim to fame was its combination of 4x4 and all wheel steering (features shared by the Latil and a few other later vehicles), and the fact that it was one of the earliest specialised vehicles to be mass produced.

The Thomas B Jeffery Co of Kenosha, Wisconsin, introduced the Quad in 1913 as a rival to the FWD Model B of 1912. The firm had previously been known for its Rambler cars and in 1916 it was acquired by Charles W Nash, who had headed Buick in 1910 and was President of General Motors from 1912. He renamed the Jeffery Quad the Nash Quad in 1917 and in the first full year turned out no less than 11,500, a figure which made Nash the world's largest truck producer. Such a specialised vehicle was seldom bought by civilian transport men and Nash abandoned it in 1928, by which time a grand total of 41,674 had been sold.

The firm merged with Kelvinator, the refrigerator maker, in 1937 and, in 1954, with Hudson to create American Motors Corporation. The new group returned to the 4x4 market in 1970 with the acquisition of the Kaiser Jeep Corporation and, as well as making

Jeeps today, produces larger military trucks under the AMC name.

To cope with the vast demand in the Great War, Quads were produced in the Paige, National, Hudson and Jeffery factories. As far as is known, all had Buda four cylinder petrol engines, originally of 3¾ x 5¼ inch bore and stroke and 32 bhp, but later with 4¼ x 5½ and 36 bhp. They had four speed and reverse gearboxes incorporating a self-locking differential from which drive was taken by shaft to bevel boxes mounted on the identical front and rear dead beam axles. Drive to the wheels was by independent shafts to rim gears in the hubs. The four wheel steering gave the 10ft 4ins wheelbase truck a similar turning circle (45 feet) to a conventional 4x2 two wheel steered truck and was necessary because of the limited degree of steering angle practicable on each set of universal driving joints. A very advanced feature was the use of drum brakes on all four wheels worked in conjunction with a transmission brake by the hand lever and on their own by the foot pedal. Another unusual feature at a time of wooden wheels on American trucks was the use of nickel-vanadium steel castings for the wheels, which were each estimated to save 40 lbs compared with wood.

Further self-locking differentials were incorporated in each bevel box. These were highly ingenious and worked on the principle that a worm wheel incorporated in each could drive a worm but not *vice versa*. They were invented by a Mr Muehl who, despite his German name, was a supplier to several American truck factories.

The Quad was rated as a two tonner but frequently carried more and towed trailers as well, being rated in finest tractor terms with 'Four Mule Power'.

It will be very interesting to see Richard Peskett's 1915 (4016B) example when restored and it is nice to know that yet another apparently extinct type of truck has survived, especially when it is one from such an interesting background, with such an unusual specification.

As a footnote, it is interesting to learn that Charles T Jeffery (Thomas Jeffery's son?) was on his way to launch the Quad on the British market (at £750 per truck) on the *Lusitania* when it was torpedoed in 1915. After 3½ hours in the sea he was rescued by a trawler and so had a luckier escape than A H Norris Perry, who had recently left Napier to import Pierce-Arrows and was drowned in the disaster.

THE GLASGOW GTZ's

**The heavy electric vehicle achieved some pockets of success
between the wars. One of the best known exponents was
the famous steam engineering firm of Richard Garrett and Sons
and here R A WHITEHEAD tells the story of their specialised GTZ
refuse collectors. With the help of contemporary engineers
and operators he recounts the trials and tribulations
that were entailed in their design construction, and eventual use.**

THE Glasgow city authorities - both elected members and their officers - had been dissatisfied with the methods of refuse collection in the city areas south of the Clyde even before the 1914-18 War. Indeed, a committee had been set up as early as 1912 to investigate the problems of the area and to suggest courses of action, but the war had intervened before anything positive had happened. It was not until well into the twenties that the matter was again tackled by the appointment of a second committee. The members of this further body visited disposal works in some of the major cities of Europe and, as a result of their studies, formulated a report by which the Corporation were advised to set up a processing plant to screen out metals from the refuse, crush and burn the residue in a power station fuelled solely on refuse and utilise the resultant clinker as an aggregate for making concrete flags and kerbs.

These proposals were adopted virtually as presented and the resultant plant was constructed on a difficult site at Craigton Road, Govan - the largest of its type in Europe and a model plant for its purpose, using mechanical means as far as possible for handling the refuse and giving an output of 10,000 kilowatts. Concurrently with this disposal reorganisation, the Corporation set in hand investigation of means whereby it might improve and mechanise the methods of collection of domestic refuse. The direction of this part of the reorganisation scheme was put in the hands of Mr W Greig, the Cleansing Superintendent, and deputed by him in turn to his able lieutenant Colin Macfarlane. Because refuse collection in this largely tenement area of Glasgow was done mostly at night, Macfarlane decided early that his new vehicles were to be electric both for silence and for ease of slow movement control, as well as for the

essential economy of using current generated from refuse, but although the Corporation already ran a fleet of twenty-two, including two 1920 Garrett 2½ ton end tippers, none fulfilled the postulates he had formulated.

Firstly he wanted a loading line no higher than 4ft 6ins to 4ft 9ins. Secondly, he required his vehicles to carry 14 cubic yards of refuse, the weight of which would vary between perhaps 4½ and 6½ tons according to area and time of year, mostly below the loading line, and thirdly he required good performance characteristics - a turning circle of fifty feet or less, a loaded speed of 12 mph when running to the disposal plant from the last pick-up and the ability to run 40 miles between charges. In addition, the

Eighteen of the initial batch of GTZs in front of the works power station at Leiston awaiting despatch to Glasgow.

The Royal party and Glaswegian dignitaries at the opening of the Govan destructor plant on 27th April 1928, with the tall figure of Prince George, afterwards Duke of Kent, in the centre and a line-up of five GTZs on the right.

Four empty vehicles descending the ramp from the destructor plant, itself a major step forward in the utilisation of refuse, which is only today being seriously revived in an effort to save raw materials.

bodies were to be side tippers. Nothing then on offer in electric vehicles came anywhere near Macfarlane's requirements but they were, nevertheless, made the basis of the conditions under which tenders were invited for the thirty-six vehicles required. Macfarlane calculated that the potential order, which would amount to close on £40,000.00, would attract considerable interest amongst manufacturers. Justifiable though his belief appeared to be, it turned out not to be correct.

In February 1926 Jack Simpson, one of the works engineers at Leiston Works, who had, more or less by accident, become involved in selling electric vehicles, was sent for by Colonel Garrett, who outlined to him the Glasgow requirements. 'I believe,' he remarked to Jack, 'that we can get an order here if we handle the matter right. Go to Glasgow, meet Macfarlane and see how it can be done'.

Jack arranged to meet Macfarlane on the Friday, travelled to Glasgow, and spent most of the day in discussing and sizing up the problem and the whole of the evening till the small hours drinking with the Deputy Superintendent. Macfarlane could see off most men as a whisky drinker, but did not defeat Jack - perhaps the first step by the latter towards the high esteem in which he was to come to be held. Macfarlane, never a patient man, had been irritated beyond measure by the defeatism and 'take-it-or-leave-it' attitudes of the major makers and found Jack's acceptance that his performance specification was a real requirement and not a vague statement of an ideal a refreshing difference of attitude.

Jack Simpson broke his journey home on the Saturday at his parents-in-law's home in Lancashire where his wife Lilian was on a visit, borrowed his mother-in-law's pastry board as a drawing board and roughed out some ideas as to how the design might be worked out. What he drew convinced him that it could be done. His report to Colonel Garrett was, 'The man knows what he wants and is determined to have it. It can be done and no one else is trying'. His outline of how he proposed to go about it was greeted with scepticism by the two other directors present, Bennett and Leggett, but Jack remained adamant that it could be done provided he was allowed the full use of the services of A J Serve, the incurably pessimistic but extremely able French electric vehicle draughtsman then working on the design of the Garrett trolleybuses. Serve had been previously with Silvertown and had a deep knowledge of electric vehicles. At first, as was his wont, he threw up his hands at the impossibility of the task in the time available, but soon he and Jack were deep in debate as to how the latter's outlines, worked out largely on intuition, could be translated into practice.

An early problem was the shape of battery which the design required. Garretts normally used Chloride batteries, but no existing Chloride design fitted the available space and the makers showed no enthusiasm for producing a special for such a small order. Jack spent a frustrating day phoning battery makers, none of whom seemed to have any interest in the work he was offering. Probably the word had been put around that the Glasgow requirements were

impossible to fulfil and that the whole thing was a wild goose chase. Whatever the reason, the design seemed at the point of being frustrated for want of the right battery when someone suggested phoning Tudor, at that time considered a Second Eleven maker, at Dukinfield. Jack asked them on the phone if they could do him batteries in the shape and properties he required. 'Lad,' came the enthusiastic response from the other end, 'for that order, we can do 'em any shape thee like'.

Finally there remained the matter of tipping. Both as to weight, and the space taken up, tipping gear on the vehicle was a nuisance, adding to the unladen weight and hence the power consumption - already a critical point. Whilst Serve was discussing this with Jack Simpson, the latter had an idea. Since the thirty-six vehicles were to tip into the same four hoppers, why go to the trouble and expense of putting tipping gear on each vehicle when eight overhead hoists at the hoppers would be capable of achieving the same objective at a saving both in capital cost and maintenance. On being sounded on the matter, Macfarlane was enthusiastic. Serve and Simpson completed their design, prepared their estimate and laid it

before Colonel Garrett. The tender, dated 3rd March 1926, for thirty-six vehicles at £1,078.0.0d each, delivered to Glasgow, was submitted and, in a letter of 24th March 1926, accepted. Jack Simpson and Serve were jubilant and Colonel Garrett was pleased but Bennett and Leggett remained sceptical that the vehicle would satisfy the performance specification as to mileage per charge.

The spring of 1926 was marred nationally by the coal strike, the General Strike and a further period of the coal strike. At Leiston there was the additional anxiety as to whether or not the new refuse collector would perform in practice as was predicted in Serve's calculations. In a letter to the Corporation written on 22nd June, Garretts suggested they complete one only in advance of the general run - to enable it to undergo on-site approval trials. This again Macfarlane approved. Serve, with aid from another Leiston electric vehicle draughtsman, Bill Dean, settled down to the slog of detailing.

The prototype was No 324 in the electric vehicle series. Work on it was completed on 25th February 1927 and it was test run over roads around the works and over the road from Leiston to Aldeburgh. Its supporters had

End-on view of three of the Garretts being tipped into the reception hoppers. The refuse handled was predominantly from the tenement areas of South Side Glasgow, and contained a relatively high proportion of coal cinders and ashes, making the tipping a dusty operation.

Close-up of the vehicle body during tipping showing the original type of body with the top openings closed in by roller shutters when not being used for loading. The shutters retracted into the central boxing when not in use. The shutters proved to be one of the more vulnerable parts of the bodies - refuse sometimes became trapped in the joints and grit from the refuse caused accelerated wear.

realised that the performance on one battery charge would be a close-run thing but the test runs at Leiston were accomplished just within the stipulations. As a result it was sent off by rail to Glasgow for its acceptance trials with Messrs Simpson and Serve travelling to meet it. With the foresight that had characterised his actions all through, Jack Simpson took Serve with him on a test run over the actual terrain on which the wagon was to work. Jogging through the daytime traffic of south side Glasgow, it horrified them by producing a mileage wildly short of the 40 specified. Once again Jack's presence of mind did not fail him. They recharged the batteries, waited until late in the evening, and then tried it over the sparsely trafficked streets. The result was gratifying - some three miles over the minimum.

The following day he saw Colin Macfarlane and put it to him that as the lorry was for night service it was not only logical but right that the appraisal trial should be carried out at night. Possibly Macfarlane saw through the subterfuge but liked the vehicle too much to let it fail. At all events - and probably because of his advice - the Corporation agreed to allow the test to be done at night and, as a result, the vehicle acquitted itself with honour. The two Garrett men sent off a triumphant telegram to the works and retired to their hotel. Bennett and Leggett were so convinced that failure could not have been averted that they did not wait for the message and travelled up to Glasgow by the night train with the idea, as Jack Simpson put it, of 'seeing what could be salvaged from the fiasco'. Arriving tired and stiff at the hotel, they went up to find Simpson and Serve in bed celebrating their success with tankards of Guinness and champagne. Far from the day of gloom and repentance they had expected, they spent the day with Simpson and Serve as guests of honour on a round of visits and inspections, terminating in a civic dinner that evening.

No 324, finished in dreadnought grey, with the Corporation's coat of arms on the offside of the cab, was No 1 in the new fleet to work out of Govan. Its successors, Nos 2-36 inclusive, bore the consecutive works numbers 344 to 378. No 2 was delivered on 22nd December 1927 and No 36 on 16th May 1928. Meanwhile, the Govan destructor/generating station had been opened by HRH Prince George on 27th April 1928. Because of its large size, almost total mechanisation and advanced methods, it was much written about in the engineering press and the actual opening, involving a popular member of the Royal Family, was noted in the national dailies.

The completion of the first order was followed by a repeat for six more, works numbers 419 to 424. Although 419 was completed first, on 29th June 1929, it took fleet number 42 and No 420 became fleet number 37, the others following in sequence when delivered between 28th and 30th September 1929. The first built was delivered last, having been shown in the meantime at the Blackpool Cleansing Confer-

ence, where it attracted much favourable notice but no orders. In fact, the only GTZs supplied to a customer other than Glasgow were two for Paisley Corporation (Works Nos 432 and 434), delivered in September 1930, which came on the end of a further batch of four (Nos 428-431) built for Glasgow between June and September 1930. Nos 435-438 for Glasgow followed in July and August 1931, bring the fleet numbers to fifty.

By this time the financial affairs of Leiston Works were in a very shaky state and the slump was adding daily to the destruction of engineering firms. Early in 1932 it was taken over by the debenture holders and it was not until mid-year, as narrated in *Garrett 200*, that, under new owners, normal trading was resumed on a much smaller scale. Glasgow Corporation were one of the first customers and had two further GTZs (Nos 439 and 440) in March 1933. Two more (Nos 441 and 442) were delivered in January 1934, the last on solid tyres.

Since Colin Macfarlane had been promoted to the post of Cleansing Superintendent, he had taken a look at the method of conducting the collecting of household refuse with a view to better utilisation of plant. One of the arguments put forward in favour of petrol engined units

was that they could be double manned, for night use in the congested inner city areas and day use in the suburbs, whereas this could not be done with electrics owing to the need to recharge the batteries. On the other hand he did not wish to sacrifice the benefit of the silence of the electric for night work nor, for that matter, the advantage of using the current from their own generators. The accessibility of the battery stand on the GTZs suggested either to him or, possibly, to someone on his staff, the idea of putting the batteries into a demountable battery crate, offloading them by crane at the end of the night shift, substituting a crate of recharged batteries and sending the vehicle off for a day's work. The policy began to be implemented in 1934. No 442 was the last made with non-detachable batteries, and numbers 443 to 445 (ordered in the autumn of 1934), designed to comply fully with the 1934 Road Traffic Act, had not only detachable battery crates but also, for the first time, pneumatic tyres. Their only drawback was an unladen weight of 5 tons 4½ cwt. Originally it was intended to fit 38ins x 8ins tyres, but difficulties with clearances on the bodywork and reluctance to raise the loading line led, in the end, to 36ins x 8ins being used. The bodywork, too, was varied to an all-over

This picture, taken outside the electric vehicle garage at Govan, shows the second design of bodywork with all-over roof and rubber strip side curtains in conjunction with flaps which were lowered during loading and raised for travelling. With heavy household refuse the vehicle was fully laden weightwise when full to the loading line, but with shop refuse, where the bulk to weight ratio was much higher, the volume under the roof enabled old boxes and light refuse to be stacked in without being blown away in transit.

roof design with rubber strip curtains for dust prevention.

The drivers complained of the steering on these three vehicles being stiff because of the resistance of the tyres at the comparatively low road speeds. McConnell, the supervisor of the Govan garage, suggested that lowered gear ratios in the steerage heads was the answer. His choice was a reduction from 11 to 1 (as supplied) to 15 to 1, but in fact, on the suggestion of Leslie Farrow, a ratio of 13 to 1 was offered and adopted, which solved the problem.

These modifications were carried through into a further batch of four (Works Nos 446-449 inclusive), supplied in 1936. Change of policy was, however, in the air at Glasgow. Arthur Bambrough, the General Manager of Leiston Works, had paid a visit to Colin Macfarlane at his office in Glasgow on 21st November 1935 in company with A R (Reg) King, his deputy and, ultimately, successor, at Leiston, during which Macfarlane had outlined to them his ideas on future vehicle requirements by his department for the financial year beginning on 1st June 1936. He had seen, and been impressed by, the Scammell Mechanical Horse and was looking for proposals based upon a five or six wheeled

articulated design using a compact tractor unit and having a load capacity of about 10 cubic yards (3 tons) but he also had ideas for a four wheeled rigid vehicle of about that capacity, roughly equivalent to a scaled-down GTZ. The fleet included a number of old type Edison three ton electrics with end tipping which had become life-expired and he was doubtless considering replacements for these, but he also had in contemplation the replacement of the existing horse-drawn vehicles used for collecting street litter.

Garretts dutifully and hopefully prepared general arrangement drawings and estimates for both types, which Bambrough delivered in person to Macfarlane on 15th April 1936. They were not successful on this occasion, however, and Metropolitan Vickers, who had come onto the electric vehicle scene in 1934, got the order. Garretts did, however, succeed, in the autumn of 1936, in selling Glasgow four further GTZs which incorporated more drastic revisions of design intended to reduce the unladen weight to bring it within the 5 ton limit and thereby qualify for £25.00 a year less in Road Fund Tax. Macfarlane had complained to Bambrough that those 4½ cwt per vehicle were costing him £100.0.0d a year in tax. Bambrough, in turn,

consulted Leslie Farrow, who predicted confidently that they could be refined out of the design. With the help of Ernest Cuthbert, later to be a director of the firm, he examined every component, stripping the weight off pound by pound, and the re-designed vehicle eventually clocked in at a half hundredweight under the 5 ton limit. Not only, of course, was there a saving in road tax but also an improvement in the mileage from each battery charge. The opportunity was also taken to incorporate a number of modifications suggested by Glasgow. Corporation, mostly arising from McConnell's experience of maintaining the earlier vehicles. Visually the most evident part of the re-design was a new cab designed to give a more modern appearance than the old pattern which dated, almost unchanged, from 1927. The new cab had raked windscreen, rounded salient angles and fully glazed doors on both driver's and mate's sides - where the old cabs had had a fixed side, latterly with glass, next to the driver and a waist-high door, with no glass, on the other side. It also had an improved front axle, Ransome and Marle's roller bearings on the prop shaft and, in keeping with the period, trafficators.

As it turned out, these four electrics were the last supplied by Garretts to Glasgow - or, indeed, any other authority - though they supplied replacement bodies for the earlier vehicles, a subject to which we will return later on. Competition for electric sales had become much more effective. Electricars Ltd of Birmingham, who had taken over the Edison electric vehicle business in the United Kingdom, had absorbed Electromobile of Otley, Yorks, in 1933 and had gone on to become one of the constituents of Associated Electric Vehicle Manufacturers in 1936. Metropolitan Vickers Electrical Co Ltd of Trafford Park, Manchester, had commenced building electrics in 1934. Victor Electrics, of Burscough Bridge, near Ormskirk, Lancashire, which began in the 1920s as the brain child of a Southport baker by building electrics on extended Model T Ford chassis, were also hankering after Glasgow work, though a vehicle of the Glasgow proportions would have been a special for them, larger than their general production run which ran up to a maximum of some 30 cwt carrying capacity. All three tendered for similar, though not identical, vehicles to the GTZ, and all of the tenders were cheaper than Garretts'. Based upon an order for four vehicles the prices tendered were:

	Electricars	£911 each
Victor	£1,077 each	
Metrovick	£1,099 each	
Garrett	£1,350 each	

Worse for all four, however, was the competition from the petrol engined camp. In 1937 Glasgow were able to buy two articulated refuse vehicles consisting of Morris-Commercial units - Brockhouse trailers for only £604.0.0d each.

On 19th November 1937 Colin Macfarlane

was in London with his son and a party of friends and colleagues - Bailie Crawford, Branks (the Glasgow Air Raid Precautions Officer), Catermole of Tudor Accumulators and a Mr Collins. Reg King, then in charge of sales but later to be general manager of Garretts, went up to London to meet them and ostensibly to discuss various points of business, notably some alterations required in eighteen replacement bodies then under construction at Garretts. As he put it, in his economical turn of phrase, 'after the usual Friday evening's entertainment' Macfarlane professed himself, probably rightly, not in a frame of mind to argue about business that evening and Reg King consequently met him again at ten o'clock the next morning. Having examined the problems of the replacement bodies, they turned to the matter which most interested King, namely, why Garretts had not received any new orders from Glasgow Corporation. With considerable regret Macfarlane explained in great detail, backed up by figures, how the sheer economics of the situation had put Garretts out of the market. The problem was basically insoluble for there was no way in which Garretts, building a batch of about four vehicles, could compete with the mass producers of motor lorries. Consequently, the GTZs supplied in 1937 were the last road vehicles made by Garretts though they continued to build specialised tractors for off-road use.

Nevertheless, the GTZ fleet already at work gave very good service and remained in use, more or less intact, until the latter fifties, by which time, despite very thorough general repairs at the Corporation's engineering works at St Rollox, the effects of twenty-five to thirty years service were beginning to be apparent. Moreover, changes in electricity generation, consequent upon nationalisation, had affected the economics of the Govan destructor plant which was approaching the age when its renewal had to be considered. The Corporation decided against renewal and the works was closed in 1960, removing by its departure one of the props of the electric vehicle fleet. The final consideration, however, was the increasing bulk to weight ratio of refuse, because of the decline of the domestic grate in which, in earlier years, so much light refuse had been burned and which had, in its turn, contributed a considerable volume of coal cinders to the refuse. This change in refuse characteristics meant that to obtain anything like a full load, in weight terms, compactor vehicles had to be used. Consequently, the GTZs were finally phased out until the last unit, Fleet No 57 (Works No 445 of 1935) was withdrawn in 1964, bringing the saga to a close.

The power unit of the GTZ was a 12hp motor designed for the purpose by Garrett's associate in the AGE combine - Bull Motors Ltd of Stowmarket. The frame and brackets were of cast steel and the armature shaft revolved in ball and roller bearings. Because it was mounted low down between the chassis side members and correspondingly exposed to road dirt and wet, the makers were requested to give particular attention to the seals and, so far as is known, they were very successful in this and no trouble was reported with motors from first to last. A short prop shaft, with Hooke joints each end, took the drive to an underslung worm on the rear axle assembly which incorporated a four pinion differential. Running voltage for journeys from depôt to collecting area and *vice versa* was 80/85 volts but a change-over switch was provided by which the two halves of the battery could be run in parallel, reducing the voltage to about 40 for slow running during street collection. In practice this was found to be less essential than anticipated and when the switch was found to be in the way of the

demountable battery crates later introduced, it was done away with without detriment to the usefulness or adaptability of the vehicles.

The chassis, as a pressed item in high tensile steel, was a bought-in component, the first twenty being supplied by Macintosh for the unbelievably low price of *£21.2s.0d* per set, though they declined further orders at that price and the immediately subsequent vehicles had frames by Rubery Owen at *£50.0s.0d* a set. The overall nett cost, incidentally, of the first ten vehicles was £8,747.0.0d (£847 each) compared with an estimated cost of £884.0.0d. The second batch of ten worked out rather better (£810.0.0d each) and even after the setback of the Rubery Owen chassis price, the third batch came out only at £840.0.0d each against, in each case, a selling price of £1,070.0.0d, the margin of £230 in the latter case being required to cover works overheads (calculated at 100% on the labour content, ie, in this case, £135) and profit which thus worked out at £95 per vehicle.

The controller was a foot-operated EMB unit giving eight speeds in each direction and was interlocked with the brakes so that the application of either hand or foot brake put the controller back to neutral. Despite the fact that the brakes operated only on the rear wheels,

they never gave rise to complaint, though by the sixties this marked the GTZ as obsolete. When the design of the final batch was under consideration there was a tentative proposal, not adopted, to use Lockheed hydraulic brakes.

Early bodies had open tops covered, when travelling, by roller shutters, which retracted into a central blind box along the spine of the body during loading but subsequent bodies had an all-over roof, the side loading apertures being fitted with rubber strip curtains and side shutters to hinge up when each compartment was full. Earlier versions had sides which hinged for emptying purposes at the loading line but in the final four vehicles the sides were arranged to hinge from the roof in two sections which saved refuse draping itself on the centre rail.

Changing over the GTZs to pneumatic tyres, superficially an easy matter, almost foundered over the matter of securing sufficient clearance in the wheel arches of the body to allow the body to be tipped and also to give clearances that would enable a wheel to be changed. Whereas, in the design of body for the solid tyred chassis, the body frame could be cranked in the horizontal plane round the back of the wheel, it was no longer possible to do this with pneumatics as it would have cut into the top inside edge of the

tyre on tipping. The problem was overcome by Leslie Farrow of the Leiston drawing office - later Garretts' chief design engineer - by making the wheel arch a steel fabrication forming part of the body frame. This essential design step, together with modifications to the front and rear hubs gave just sufficient clearance but it was a close thing. The conversion kits designed by Garretts were incorporated into the vehicles at each major overhaul at the Corporation's St Rollox works and, by bringing them into compliance with the 1934 Road Traffic Act, extended what would otherwise have been limited lives.

The earlier vehicles, running on solid tyres over sett roadways, took a considerable pounding which led to failures of welds on light fabricated items such as framework to the circuit breakers and switchboard and flexing of the composite wood and steel framing of the cabs though once pneumatics were introduced there was much less trouble with such items.

It is curious how annoyances nearly always arise from minor slips. For instance, in the slow running and battery change-over switches the copper contacts were mounted on 3/8in copper studs through which the current passed. The switches were a bought-in item and one supplier

made the economy of substituting steel for copper studs, with the result that overheating and charring of the insulation occurred - a classic illustration of the truth behind the axiom 'penny wise, pound foolish' so often dismissed as a cliché. Considering that the GTZs were a twenties design and that, for their last thirty years, they were double manned so as to work round the clock, their immunity from serious troubles was remarkable.

When they were new, Glasgow Corporation assigned them a life expectancy of fifteen years. In fact, most of them achieved about thirty. Like the trams and the underground they became part of the fabric of the Glasgow scene, looked upon by those who drove and maintained them with the same wry affection as that which inspired the underground staff by infinite ingenuity and resource to keep their seventy and eighty year old charges running. Time had, inexorably, run out for all the Glasgow electric rolling stock, though it is a matter of regret that, so low was the preservation interest in battery electrics at the time, No 57, probably the last big battery electric of its generation to run in revenue earning service, was allowed to end up as scrap. The tide of opinion and fashion in the fifties and sixties was running strongly for

The final batch of four under erection at Town Works, Leiston. It had been hoped that this revised and lightened design might be the basis of future Glasgow purchasing policy, but the low capital cost of i/c vehicles, compared with electrics, turned the attention of the Cleansing Committee away from electrics. Five years later, with wartime fuel rationing, the electric was back in favour, only to fade away again with plentiful supplies of motor fuel in the fifties. By then Glasgow had adopted S&D vehicles.

motors and the oil based economy. Had the same decisions to be taken in the 1980s, what might the answer have been? Few in the mid-fifties would have said that fifteen years later the Glasgow underground would have had a rebirth. Perhaps, had the cards fallen out differently, electricity generated in a large version of Govan power station might yet have supplied current to a fleet of trams, trolleybuses and electric lorries.

BERNARD
THE PERFECT ATHLETE

**For as long as he can remember, MARTIN D PHIPPARD has been
fascinated by the handsome French Bernard trucks and has spent years
trying to discover the elusive history of its makers.
He has paid several visits to France to talk to operators
and others involved with the firm and has even placed
a half page advertisement appealing for information in *Le Poids Lourd*.
As this netted only one reply, one can understand his difficulty
in tracing the complete story, but what follows is everything
that he has been able to track down to date of their interesting story.**

THE idea of perfection is simplicity itself, its realisation infinitely more difficult. Yet there are those who, throughout their lives, tirelessly seek the goal of perfection, constantly looking ahead for better things. One such man was Edouard Bernard, a commercial vehicle builder who, from the very earliest days of his career, turned his back on mediocrity and, as a result, gave rise to one of France's most respected trucks, the Bernard.

Edouard Bernard was 31 years old and a tipping gear manufacturer when he first entered into the competitive world of truck building. The year was

Long distance haulage had always been the domain of Bernard vehicles and clearly this 1947 model operated by Georges Borca was destined to get around a bit. By this period Bernard trucks carried the 'athlete' emblem on the radiator as well as the Bernard name inside a chrome oval. Diesel power had been standardised on since 1935 and Michelin tyres became standard equipment two years later.

1923 and by that time the idea of motorised vehicles was well established in the minds of all but the most sceptical haulage company owners. But certain areas had been neglected and one of these was the field of tipper work. Not only were horses still used to haul loads of material for road building projects, but the operation of tipper gear was still very much a manual task requiring lots of winding in order to raise or lower the waggon body.

The very real need for a motor driven vehicle with a power tipper was obvious to Edouard Bernard and, as a result, his début into the market centred around just such a machine, which had been under development since 1918. Exhibited at the 1923 Paris Salon and featuring a proprietary 14hp 2.6 litre side valve petrol engine with a Solex carburettor, a four speed (plus reverse) gearbox, double reduction rear axle, four wheel brakes, pneumatic tyres and a Técalemit chassis lubrication system, but no cab, the first Bernard vehicle set the standard by which all subsequent models were measured. Stylish and compact, the tipper was equipped with two underfloor hydraulic rams which could raise the all-steel 1500kg capacity two cubic metre body to an angle of 45 degrees. Other advantages of the Bernard tipper included the low loading height (which made hand loading a much simpler task), an automatic tail gate and the famous 'one year guarantee' that was to stay with Bernard vehicles until the very last one was produced. Electric lights were also offered as optional equipment on the first Bernard. Larger 2 and 3 tonne tippers followed in 1925, and by 1927 dozens of Bernards were in operation, not only in Paris and its environs (Bernards were built in the Arcueil suburb) but as far afield as the Loire. Testimonials of the day, written by satisfied Bernard customers, include some that state that they had been able to give up using horses entirely! Most praised the rugged reliability of the Bernard and its tipper body. A larger 3.3 litre engine had been introduced in 1926 and in the same year a special high speed coach was built, this having a six cylinder side valve engine initially from America. Coach building was to become an important part of the Bernard empire, although in the final 10 years of operation coaches disappeared from the scene, leaving design engineers free to concentrate

The picture and the sign say it all. Prize-winning Bernard, in classic style of 1949.

Six wheelers had been built by Bernard since 1936 and in appearance this 1949 model 18 tonner [150 MB19 CA653] was not a great deal different from the earliest models. However, power was a 150hp diesel, drive axle was hub reduction type and tare weight had been reduced in an effort to produce maximum payload.

on the vital task of manufacturing more powerful engines and even more luxurious cabs.

The Bernard range had grown considerably by 1929 following the introduction of fresh capital a year earlier, when Camions Bernard was formed as a limited liability company, and its range extended to eight different chassis/cabs, these having straight and low frames and either four or six cylinder engines producing 14hp, 16hp or 22hp and now actually made by Bernard. Gross vehicle weights ran from 3.8 tonnes to six tonnes and electric starting and lighting was now standard equipment on six cylinder chassis and an extra cost option on the four cylinder models.

In addition to normal road vehicles, Bernard also offered several special types for the new high speed services in which road transport was just beginning to make real progress, much to the consternation of the railways. Coaches were also offered, as were the now well established Bernard

machines than the A6SRs, on the Paris to Nantes route, serving towns such as Angers, Le Mans and St Nazaire. Drouin Frères, whose operation was to grow to become one of the largest in France, continued to buy and operate Bernard vehicles until the manufacturer finally stopped production. They also operated many coaches, including the beautiful B6S CL, a 4.5 tonne gvw 25-35 seater first produced in 1930 and a vehicle which was to look ahead of its time in terms of styling even a decade later. Among the instruments provided on the B6S CL were a coolant temperature gauge and an odometer, refinements indeed for the 1930s!

Open touring coaches with four doors along each side were also built in 1930, these being designated the B4SA. Other versions included the 'short luxury' coach and the A6SC, a model which had first appeared in 1928 and which, in that year, had been awarded the coveted first prize for 'overall style and comfort' in a national competition sponsored by the French trade press association. Unquestionably, the diversification was helping to enlarge Bernard's reputation as a quality vehicle builder but one cannot help but consider the contradiction in its slogan of the time which was 'Do one thing, but do it well'.

During the latter part of the 1920s and throughout the 1930s, the diesel engine was to obtain an increasingly strong foothold as the power plant for trucks and coaches. Bernard, in common with Berliet and Citroën, was anxiously watching the success (or failure) of various types of diesel in 1930 and in 1931 set up a brief liaison with CLM Diesels of Lille, who built a high speed two stroke under licence from Junkers. However, the relationship was as unsuccessful as it was short lived, with neither Bernard nor CLM deriving any benefit at all from the deal.

Undeterred by the failure to get into diesel power right at the start, Edouard Bernard, in 1932, developed a 6804cc (95x120mm) 8 cylinder petrol engine capable of the high output from a side valve unit for its day of 150 bhp.

The new, high speed Bernard F8

tippers which were available with three cubic metre bodies.

A trade press periodical dated May 1929 described the 3.5 tonne payload Bernard Six as 'an excellent example of design and management at their best'. Little wonder: every driver knows just how difficult it is today to maintain high average speeds yet, unbelievably, over 50 years ago Bernard trucks were running the 515 miles between Marseilles and Paris in 18 hours and thereby averaging an incredible 28.5 miles per hour! Such speeds are remarkable enough in themselves, but when one remembers the appalling road conditions of the day and the tremendous hammering the trucks must have taken, the feat is nothing short of fantastic.

The Service Rapide (SR) series was catching on in a big way and in order

to satisfy the needs of their customers, Bernard began offering sleeper cab modifications and large 500 litre (132 gallon) fuel tanks.

D Freiche-Prim, an operator specialising in the Paris-Marseilles run, openly advertised a guaranteed 24-hour service using their 16hp A6SR box vans. Interestingly, the vehicles they used featured a novel sloping cab roof which must have been extremely effective in reducing frontal wind resistance, a factor which probably contributed to the oustandingly good fuel economy achieved by the operator.

Drouin Frères of Nantes was another company which had already noticed the advantages offered by the speed and reliability of Bernard vehicles. They operated five tonne gvw B6SRs, larger, more powerful

A four tonne capacity B4-D1 of the early thirties with four cylinder 16hp petrol engine, though some had used unsatisfactory Junkers-licence two stroke diesels.

A larger six cylinder chassis of 1930 used for both high speed goods and passenger transport. The EB on the radiator was in honour of Edouard Bernard, who must have liked the comparison with that other famous EB radiator badge - Ettore Bugatti!

denied and in the following years his company went from strength to strength, finally dropping petrol engines altogether in 1935. A three cylinder version of the 70hp Gardner had been built in 1934, this reputedly returning as much as 25 mpg in service as a medium duty power plant. Bernard had taken a few liberties with the larger 100hp diesel, such as moving the fuel pump to the opposite side, a move which the always exacting people at Gardner viewed with horror and alarm!

The year 1936 was significant for Bernard for two totally unrelated reasons. Firstly, it saw the creation of the company's first six wheeler, a massive 6x2 12/15 tonne machine with the six cylinder Gardner diesel and Hispano/Rolls-Royce type servo brakes fed by twin hydraulic pumps. This was the first of a long and successful line of six wheelers the company was to produce over the next 30 years and typified the solid strength of the Bernard vehicles of that period.

The second point was that in 1936 Georges Borca quit his job as a company driver and set up as an independent owner/operator. Les Transports Borca, as his enterprise was later to become known, was another company which, like Drouin Frères, stayed loyal to the Bernard product for as long as the company remained in business. Throughout the history of Bernard, almost every Paris Salon was to see at least one and often two vehicles on the Bernard stand in the colours of either Transports Borca or Drouin Frères. And the loyalty was not misplaced. Both transport companies expected and received reliability and economy from their vehicles and each grew and prospered, thanks in part to Bernard.

The years immediately prior to the Second World War saw Bernard concentrating on vehicles with pay-loads ranging from six to 12 tonnes and on the development of their own diesel engines. These were similar in many respects to the Gardner, having top speeds in the region of 1700 or 1800 rpm and a wide operating band. As with most Bernard products their early diesels were to prove durable and economical. This remained true right up until the late 1950s at which time the company tried to expand in so many different areas at the same time that they over-stretched both their budget and their expertise. In 1939, the company produced an armoured

chassis was the one selected to house this impressive engine. It had a five speed gearbox, automatic chassis lubrication, servo brakes and the distinctive feature of a long bonnet liberally decorated at the front with the new wonder metal, chrome. The F8 was for 10 tonnes gross and capable of carrying a genuine 6½ tonne payload at up to 75 kph. At the same time, a new luxury passenger coach was built, this also having the big eight cylinder unit for power. Dual rate helper springs, dashboard lights and good driver environment were among the features of the F8 and the luxury coach which obviously made quite an impression with the trade press of the period. One journalist, in 1932, wrote that he could tell that Bernard wanted to serve its customers well. 'Certain truck builders,' he continued, 'left the worry of inade-

quate performance or premature breakdowns to the customer. Bernard was not like that'.

Either by sheer good fortune or clever guesswork, Bernard eventually managed to latch on to what was probably the best diesel engine available at the time, the legendary British Gardner. This was first installed in Bernard chassis in 1933, at which time Bernard obtained a manufacturing licence for the 70hp four cylinder and 100hp six cylinder versions. The difficult diesel hurdle had been crossed, an especially significant fact when one remembers the enormous difficulties being faced at the same time by Berliet, whose licence-built Saurer 'Acro' diesels were initially far from successful.

That Edouard Bernard was delighted with the reliability and economy of his new diesels cannot be

Paris Auto Salon of 1951 provided a unique opportunity to investigate the difference bodywork could make to a truck. Short wheelbase, very old fashioned looking vehicle in centre contrasts strongly with the Borca tractor on the right.

Bernard vehicles were often shown at exhibitions without the engine side covers, giving visitors a chance to look over the superb engineering. Radiator shell had, by this time, assumed the size and shape that was to make Bernard stand out from all other French vehicles.

tractor that was steered using an unusual articulated frame method (similar to current bucket loaders) but the vehicle was experimental and production was not taken up.

The war years saw development of nearly all kinds severely curtailed for Bernard which, along with Delahaye, Laffly, Unic, Simca and La Licorne, joined the GFA group in an effort to keep up some sort of sales presence during German occupation. Nowadays, of course, Unic is the only manufacturer surviving under its own name, although how long its autonomy will remain under the Iveco umbrella is hard to predict. Little is known about the Bernards which took part in the war except that when the Germans arrived, the vehicles they favoured for the really tough work were the Bernard and the Willème, two rugged old beasts of burden which had undergone roughly parallel lines of development although, of course, Willème had specialised in extra heavy haulage.

After the war, heavy duty four and six wheelers continued to be the main line of production although coaches were still manufactured and were offered by Bernard until the mid-

1950s. Six cylinder diesels (8.4 litres) were the normal power plant, though a four cylinder 5.6 litre diesel was available from 1948. The option of full air brakes was also just around the corner.

Tractors for artic work were added to the growing Bernard range in 1949, as were truck and drawbar trailer combinations, these having gross weights extending to 21 tonnes. In addition there was a 12 tonne gvw tipper and several 4x2 and 6x2 rigids with weights to 18 tonnes gvw. Michelin tyres had become standard equipment and the first hub-reduction driving axles were introduced to the heavier trucks in the range. Another important development was that of low tare weights and Bernard made strides in this direction by producing an 18 tonne gvw rigid six wheeler which, when powered by the Bernard

150 MB, 12.1 litre Bernard diesel and equipped with a huge, high sided stake and rack body, weighed in at under seven tonnes tare. Bernard was to excel in this area and, by 1953, had built a rigid four wheeler that weighed in at well under four tonnes and yet grossed out at nearly 13 tonnes. By 1954, weight-saving aluminium chassis rails were being offered by Bernard, an advanced feature seldom found today outside North America.

Looking at the sheer size and ruggedness of the post-war rigid six wheelers with their hub-reduction drive axles, beautiful coach work and ornate chrome embellishments, it is easy to see how Edouard Bernard conceived the new emblem for his trucks which was 'Le coeur et les muscles de l'athlete complet' or 'The heart and muscles of the perfect athlete'. This strong, yet highly

Several clever embellishments made the Bernard a very distinctive truck. This tidy four wheeler, operated by a high speed operator almost 30 years after the first high speed French road hauliers started business in the late 20s, shows off the famous chrome radiator shell, chrome and rubber strips on the front bumper, around the van body and above the windscreen, and an oddly shaped window behind the driver. Bodywork in this instance was by Jean Chereau of Avranches.

appropriate emblem was to grace the front of each Bernard forthwith.

Another Bernard move about 1950 was to keep the loading height as low as possible by locating the rear axle(s) through oval holes cut in the chassis side rails. Their 6x2 low height Porte Char or tank transporter chassis was to gain popularity with low loader operators for obvious reasons.

Visitors to the Paris Salon in 1951 were treated to an unbelievably varied display of vehicles on the Bernard stand. In addition to the usual chassis/cabs (minus bonnet covers in order that the now famous Bernard diesels could be inspected), there were several four and six wheelers, each with a highly individualistic cab which had been built, presumably, by the body builders.

For example, Drouin Frères had a large box van on show, this having a correspondingly large cab, while La Mure, who operated oil tankers, exhibited a six wheeler tanker with a small, almost claustrophobic cab. Sandwiched between the Drouin and La Mure trucks was a small chassis/cab with a styling reminiscent of early 1930s Bernards while, in complete contrast, on the far side of the La Mure tanker stood one of Borca's splendid tractor/trailer combinations, this featuring styling that was far ahead of its time.

There is no denying that the G Borca et Fils (as the company had now become) exhibit marked yet another major chapter in Bernard's history. The Bernard tractor was the fore-runner of many similar models to be seen later in prestige-conscious fleets such as Borca's. It had long flowing lines, making it wonderfully aero-dynamic, fully closed-in rear

wheels and back of chassis and was coupled to a handsome Fruehauf aluminium box van semi-trailer with long radiused front corners. In short, the Borca Bernard looked as out of place among the boxy, bulbous trucks on almost every other stand as did its successor, the Charbonneaux-cabbed Bernard, which first appeared almost a decade later. Borca used a number of similar Bernard/Fruehauf combinations to haul a mobile General Motors 'Frigidaire - Tomorrow's Kitchen' exhibit around the country in 1957 and even at that time the tractors looked remarkably modern.

But if 1951 was a good year in many respects, it was a sad one in others. For it was in 1951 that Edouard Bernard died, leaving the responsibility of the company and of trying to achieve perfection, to his young son Raymond. Edouard Bernard was only 59 when he died and it is probable that had he survived another decade, Bernard vehicles would still be built

Interior shot of early sixties cabover shows the tremendous amount of room available. Passenger's seat is a high-back type with arm rests, underneath which was a large toolbox. The two-stick gearbox was to stay with Bernard until the end and was the one source of criticism levelled at the manufacturer by a journalist from the French periodical *Le Poids Lourds* who, when testing a tractor unit, said that a single gear lever with a splitter button should replace the now obsolescent two-stick arrangement. The date of the test was 1962.

Taken in 1960, this picture shows a Drouin Frères Bernard tractor loading one of the flat bottom pleasure craft used to transport passengers in comfort along the Seine on sightseeing excursions.

today. As it was, Raymond was just too young and inexperienced to take on the job left open to him, although this was not to make itself obvious until five or six years later, at which time the company found itself, uncharacteristically, in trouble.

But whatever Raymond Bernard lacked in experience, he certainly tried to make up for in innovation and hard work. Very soon after the untimeley death of his father, the first forward control truck in the Bernard range appeared, this being a modest nine tonne gross machine. Known as the CA 40, the vehicle was initially a non-sleeper, although the space advantage offered over the long bonneted models was soon fully utilised and a large sleeper cab was added to the range. On the CA 40 model, the entire engine (a 110hp six cylinder diesel) was ahead of the front axle and a good ride was afforded by virtue of the very long front springs. At the same time, 48-seater buses were being built, together with the MB 44, a bullet-shaped 44-seater bus with a 150hp engine and, unusual for that era, windows in the roof as well as alongside the passengers.

The Type 110 diesel was uprated to 120hp in 1954, at which time power steering became an option on heavy chassis. Two speed auxiliary gearboxes were also introduced in 1954 and Bernard began looking at turbocharging as a possible means of improving the power rating of their engines. However, the company was never to perfect the technique of turbo-charging and engines of this type were not installed in Bernard chassis until the company was taken over by Mack Trucks in the early 1960s. The ill-fated Dieselair 200, a remarkably unsuccessful turbocharged engine, was tried for a while about 1958, but was swiftly withdrawn when it was found to be unreliable.

Also in the mid-1950s, a 6x4 tipper for site work was added to the already extensive Bernard line. Some 19 tonne gvw four wheelers with engine options of either 120hp or 150hp and five or ten speed splitter gearboxes were introduced, these having shorter

Six wheeler vans were generally more common in France than in Britain during the period 1950 to 1960, particularly among refrigerated transporters. Here a 6x2 with bodywork by Jean Chereau shows off a twin headlamp arrangement and yet another oddly shaped window to the rear of the driving position.

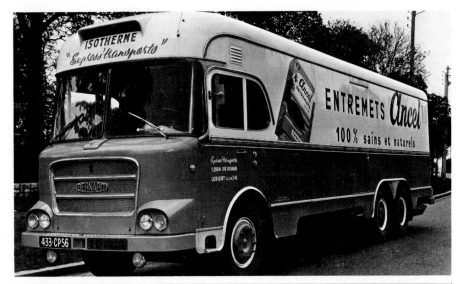

Probably the most expensive and least successful vehicle ever built by Bernard was this impressive 8x4 rigid operated by AEM Frigo. The truck had several interesting features, including the new Dunlop 'Pneuride' air suspension system and a Telma retarder. Unfortunately, unladen weight was only a shade under 15 tonnes and though the unit was designed to operate at 33 tonnes gvw, the French authorities refused to issue operating authority for any more than 26 tonnes gvw, classifying the vehicle as a 6x4! Beautiful and rare it may have been, but a payload of 11 tonnes only made the vehicle impractical and it was subsequently sold at a remarkably low mileage to the French manufacturer, Unic.

snouts and being termed by Bernard as 'semi forward control' vehicles. Six wheelers were, by this time, rated at 26 tonnes gvw and tractors at 35 tonnes gcw. Forward control was offered on almost any truck in the range, the 6x4 tipper being the notable exception, and the curious central-cab steel carrier, Bernard's ugliest truck without a doubt, joined the ranks in either 4x2 or 6x2 form.

Although, as already mentioned, the late 1950s were to mark the gradual decline of Bernard's finances and fortunes, there was certainly little indication of this in the vehicles being turned out from the company's premises in Arcueil. The bonneted four and six wheelers were classically proportioned and styled and the forward control models featured cabs which were the envy of every other manufacturer. After all, how many builders, more than 20 years ago, offered on the list of options such equipment as 'high back passenger seat - with armrests' or 'full wrap-around windscreen for unrestricted vision'?

The ultimate in sleeper cabs? This exquisite 6x2 refrigerated transporter must surely have been an owner-operator machine boasting, as it does, a sleeper cab area large enough to hold a party in! Although built in 1964 when Bernard was technically part of the Mack Trucks organisation, this model was a real Bernard. Bodywork, as may be expected, was by Pelpel, whose scrupulous attention to detail may be seen in the fairing round the roof-mounted air conditioner and the chrome-plated flush-mounted fold-down steps leading up to the inspection hatch. Vehicles similar to this Bernard appeared in illustrations on the joint Mack/Bernard sales literature *circa* 1964 and looked to be at least a decade ahead of the not very streamlined B-model Macks pictured on the same brochures.

Introduced by the Mack/Bernard consortium in 1964 was the TD 11, an enlarged version of the earlier bonneted Bernard. Distinctive Bernard grille and emblem was retained but was complemented by Mack logo and Bulldogs on the engine cover. Huge cab was a firm favourite with drivers of that period. This photo is by courtesy of P Davis.

Motor Panels of Coventry designed and built 30 of these distinctive cabs for Mack/Bernard in 1965. Although powered by the Mack V8 END 864 rated at 260hp and a big truck by European standards at that time, the vehicle was not well liked by drivers. Emblem on the bottom right side of cab [*lower left in photo*] reads F700 although, of course, this was not an F700 Mack cab at all.

Not quite a Charbonneaux cab, but a close copy nevertheless, was this version built by Pelpel of Rennes for the Mack/Bernard. Engine was the END 711 Mack Thermodyne and gearbox the Mack TRD 7225, a 10 speed direct drive splitter box. For Transports Borca of Paris, this vehicle represented the gradual transition from purebred Bernards to pure-bred Mack Bulldogs.

It is true to say that the biggest problem facing Bernard at this time concerned engines. Cabs were fine (and even more exotic versions were on the way in 1960), Bernard gearboxes and rear axles had always proved virtually indestructible and operators were still covered by the 'one year regardless of mileage' guarantee. But some operators were after more power than the trusty Bernard 12.1 litre in-line six cylinder engine could produce and the V8 Dieselair 200 had cost Bernard so much that the company was suffering from the old adage 'once bitten, twice shy'.

With the arrival of 1960, hopes were running high that Bernard might weather the financial storm and sail on once more into calmer waters. The extremely futuristic Philippe Charbonneaux cab (so advanced that even today it would look futuristic!) differed so radically from all previous Bernard models that it was hoped it would be some compensation for the limited range of engines. The Dunlop Pneuride air suspension system was also offered on some Bernards and was later added to every model the company built. But such advances don't come cheap and Bernard was really in no position to be investing precious capital in anything but new engines.

Engines MB 630 and later MF 630, both 12.1 litres in capacity and putting out 160hp and 165hp respectively, were joined in 1961 by a 12.6 litre in-line six, the MF 636, this being rated at 185hp. But according to several operators who tried the larger engine, it was far less reliable than was expected. However, the MB 630 which was tested by the French periodical *Le Poids Lourds* in 1961 when installed in a new Charbonneaux-cabbed tractor, was found to be effective enough at 35 tonnes gcw. In fact, the tester was prompted to write, 'a vehicle likely to succeed in every regard, of which the builder can be extremely and justifiably proud and the user supremely confident'. Such kind words, but unfortunately words didn't help enough to pull the company back from the brink of financial disaster and only two years later, in 1963, Bernard and

its new factory, still in the Seine District at Bagneux, was taken over by Mack Trucks and gradually run down until its closure in 1967. This sad fate should be set in the context of a seriously declining French heavy vehicle industry facing competition in particular from Germany.

Bernard's final years before takeover were marked by some stylish designs and limited cost saving from buying in such components as ZF twelve speed gearboxes. The startling Charbonneaux designed cab (Philippe Charbonneaux had been responsible for styling the Facel Vega and first Chevrolet Corvettes) may have been too much for Bernard's more conservative customers, but it certainly updated Bernard's rather staid image.

One of their final designs before the arrival of Mack was a rigid eight wheeler, this being a superbly modern affair with the impressive designation, 26DA 8P 180. Eight wheelers have

never been common in France and it is not really known why the operator, AEM Frigo, opted for this configuration although it is quite possible that if it were destined to haul loads of swinging meat, it would have offered more stability than an articulated vehicle.

The specification was as impressive as the designation, power coming from the MF 636 diesel (rated at 185hp). Both rear axles were hub-reduction types, these and the front axles riding on air suspension. Cab was a full sleeper with the distinctive round porthole type window behind the driving compartment and the vehicle was equipped with a Telma electro-magnetic retarder. But, unfortunately, the vehicle was doomed - the problem being simply one of weight. Both Bernard and the operator had hoped to register the truck for use at 33 tonnes gvw but the French government refused to

liked Mack's products enough to stay with them. They still buy Mack today.

Although the intervention by Mack Trucks did little to get the Bernard organisation back on its feet (and as a foothold in Europe was no more successful than AEC's contemporary liaison with Willème), the years between 1964 and 1967 saw some unusual and interesting Mack/Bernard and Mack variants emerge.

For example, an extremely handsome normal control tractor, powered by the Thermodyne END 711 diesel, appeared in 1964, this having a much larger cab than the previous models and featuring twin headlamps. Known as the TD 11, this model was a great favourite among truck drivers of the period.

Another rare version, this time a pure Mack apart from the cab, was the tractor unit powered by the END 864 V8 diesel and sporting a Motor Panels cab. Only 30 of these trucks were built, and they were rated, rather optimistically, for operation at 75 tonnes gcw under special use conditions, of course. The design was later taken up by Floors in Holland and became the Mack based FTF (still in production today in modified form as a 6x4 and 8x4 but with no Mack components).

The round-fronted Unic (Izoard) cab was also tried for a while by Mack as was a special forward control version offered by Pelpel. However, none of these was to prove successful and, by 1967, the idea of Mack drive lines housed in European style cabs was abandoned. Instead, the R series 'conventional' which replaced the ageing B series in 1965 was introduced, the cabs invariably undergoing radical enlargement at the hands of experienced body specialists such as Pelpel. This effectively drew the definitive demarcation line between what had been Mack/Bernard (later Europeanised Mack) and Mack proper. So ended a great chapter in truck history, though happily the Bernard name lives on today with a range of industrial engines whose production was taken over by Renault.

acknowledge the fourth axle and stubbornly insisted that the truck was really only a six wheeler and therefore could only gross 26 tonnes. Had the Bernard been lighter, 26 tonnes might have been acceptable, but with a tare weight of almost 15 tonnes, the 11 tonne payload was ridiculous. The Bernard eight wheeler was first registered on 22nd January 1963, shortly before Mack moved in.

Strictly speaking, the Bernard story ends in 1963. But, of course, the company was to continue, although in different form, for another three years. Mack, who never seem to be able to keep a junior partner in business for very long (look at Hayes and Brockway) at least managed to identify the Bernard problem as being mainly one of insufficiently powerful engines and promptly offered their own engines and gearboxes in Bernard chassis. The resulting vehicle, while not a true Bernard, was nevertheless a

highly successful hybrid. But it was also extremely expensive. The Bernard was never sold on price, but with the Mack drive line, the vehicle became prohibitively costly. Sales dwindled, staff deserted and finally Mack closed the doors.

People were always quick to praise the virtues of the Bernard with its 'heart and muscles of the perfect athlete' and operators such as Drouin Frères and Transports Borca witnessed the company's closure with deep regret, not only for practical but for sentimental reasons, too. For over the years the families of Bernard, Borca and Drouin had been closely associated. Drouin Frères continued to buy Bernards for as long as they were available and were impressed by the Mack drive line in the latest models. But when supplies of Bernards ran dry, they finally changed their allegiance to Saviem. Borca, meanwhile, continued similarly but

THE OTHER LONDON PALLADIUM

**Since the arrival of the motor lorry in Britain, there have been literally hundreds of rival makes vying for sales.
One of the many to be briefly popular at the time of the Great War was Palladium, whose story has been pieced together here by NICK BALDWIN with the help of JOHN M BLAND, who supplied many of the unique photographs.**

PALLADIUM Autocars Ltd was typical small assembler of cars with premises in Normand Road, West Kensington. Under the ownership and direction of Dr John Ross McMahon it bought French engines and components and, commencing in 1912, offered a range of 10, 12 and 15 horsepower four cylinder cars, joined by a six in 1915. Chapuis Dornier engines were used and Doyle lists the cars as hailing from Puteaux and Twickenham. After a time *Autocar* said that aft of the dashboard the cars were wholly British.

Based on these car chassis, an assortment of commercial bodywork was occasionally mounted and by 1913 Palladium offered 8, 12 and 20 cwt capacity vans. The firm had quite extensive Colonial sales, handled by Tozer Kemsley. John Richards, the sales manager at Palladium, picked an inauspicious moment to set out on a world sales tour in his 18/22 car in July 1914 and had to be called back to the factory to help with the reorganisation for military production and to help fight Napier over a detachable

An advertisement for the largest of the car-derived light commercials of September 1914. The slogan 'the lowest grade of any price' can hardly have been flattering!

A December 1917 advertisement giving an idea of Palladium's sales achievements and showing a typical Dorman engined YD 3-4[½] tonner.

The old 3-4 tonner was redesigned as the YEE in 1919, as shown here, and had a Continental 45 bhp four cylinder engine.

wheel patent that was claimed to have been infringed.

Car production was suspended until 1922, apart from the brief mandatory fling with the cyclecar craze, and the light commercials (including a new 3/4 elliptic sprung 10 cwt van chassis at £271 in 1914) were slowly ousted in favour of those for loads of 25 cwt and upwards. By the end of 1914 a prototype 3 to 4 tonner was nearing completion, built largely to the War Office's 3 ton Subsidy regulations in that it had military pattern artillery wheels and shock-proof radiator mounts. The 38 bhp engine with bore and stroke of 4-1/8 x 5½ inches was claimed to be by Palladium, but unless they had stopped buying French components this seems unlikely. It was certainly an unusual unit with cooling water forced in at the top of the block and hot water also

The final shape of a Palladium lorry exemplified by this 1920 demonstrator. The badge of this and all other Palladiums showed a semi-clad Grecian warrior.

Assembling YEEs in the boom years of 1919/20. On the left are a selection of the American components used - Timken axles and Continental engines.

The cluttered but modern machine shop at Felsham Road which had been installed for munitions and aero engine work and from which emerged a flat twin air cooled cyclecar engine in 1919.

drawn from the top (one hopes that it actually circulated). It also had optional dual ignition and what must have been one of the earliest electric self starters on a heavy vehicle, which cost £35 extra and worked through the specially strengthened timing gears. The cone clutch mechanism was claimed to be as on the AEC B type, as indeed was the four speed chain gearbox. It had a Kirkstall front axle and a rear axle incorporating an overhead David Brown worm. The prop shaft featured flexible joints made of rhino hide sandwiched in pigskin.

The facilities at West Kensington proved to be inadequate, even when the showroom there, which had replaced one in the Euston Road, was turned over to make more assembly space. As a result, a new works was taken over at Felsham Road, Putney Bridge, where the first truck was

completed in March 1915. By September Palladium claimed to have several months of orders for the 3-4 tonner in hand from private operators and to be able to supply their only other remaining model, the 30 cwt chassis, from stock. The necessarily short gestation period of the YA/YB/YC models (the only difference seems to have been gear ratios and tyre equipment) seem to have resulted in all sorts of hiccups in service and in December 1915 the 3-4 tonners were redesigned, ostensibly because component shortages made this essential. Out went the 'troublesome' chain box to be replaced by a spur gearbox and in came the Dorman 4JO 40hp proprietary engine, though chassis with 'standard' engines (now 4½ x 5½) were offered for a time at a saving of £65 compared with the £760 of the Dorman powered chassis. Free driver training was thrown in with these sums, a necessary precaution with so many of the nation's young men fighting abroad and lots of older men steeped in horse-drawn traditions left behind to keep the transport system running.

Amongst sizeable users of Palladiums were the distributors of Pratts Petroleum, whilst several were sold in the Bristol area by Harris and Hasell, later famous for the import of Reo commercials. Probably no more than a few hundred Palladium lorries were built before the factory switched over wholly to munitions and aero engine work in 1917/18, and indeed in 1919 the firm took the unusual step of announcing to prospective commercial vehicle customers that they should write to the factory 'even if they had received no reply before' - surely not a good sales omen! All chassis would, in future, be built to very fine tolerances and would be elaborately standardised. The machine tools were all relatively new and had been producing only 1 per cent of reject parts in the war. Once more the 3-4 tonner was redesigned, this time incorporating a Continental 4½ x 5½ inch bore and stroke engine which developed 45 bhp. It used lots of other American components too, including a Timken rear axle and a dry, multi-plate clutch. The price had now gone up to £1085 for the chassis of the YEE four

tonner, which could be differentiated from the earlier types by its more tapered bonnet. Unfortunately, by the time that the new Palladium was available in September 1919 there was only another year of the lorry sellers' market to run and thereafter prices had to be reduced year by year until in the end it was down to £695 in 1924.

In an effort to broaden sales, Palladium tried to woo the psv market with a pneumatic tyred version which featured an unusual rear suspension layout. There were two sets of springs attached to the chassis at their front ends and held together by a trunnion at their centres. The trailing ends were bolted above and below the axle which resulted in a 4 cwt saving in unsprung weight and a much smoother ride than normal. In 1923 it was still further refined so that the upper springs only came into effect when the chassis was laden. A few psv chassis were sold for double deck bodywork, notably in Cornwall and Northampton, but production was down to a trickle by 1922, when Palladium asked the technical press to refute rumours that they had gone out of business. Even if

they had not at that stage, they must have been semi-dormant on the commercial vehicle side and were never referred to again, despite appearing in buyers' guides until 1925.

Their final years were spent producing sound little cars with 11.9hp Dorman engines and a good sporting record, but even this side foundered in 1925. Afterwards there was talk of Gordon England Ltd taking over the spares to keep existing Palladiums running, but whether they did or did not, all the worldly remains of Palladium Autocars Ltd ended up with a car dealer named Jack McEwan on the Gt North Road between *The Tally Ho* and Highgate, where there was a jumble of fields, allotments and dealers' yards in those far-off days.

One of our older readers, Bert Blower, used to buy unsaleable cars from Jack McEwan, the going rate in about 1935 being £6-£10 per dozen -- once he acquired the second Alvis ever built and after running it as a hack for his scrap business he regrets to remember that it went 'to the melting pot'. Jack McEwan was on his

way up in the motor trade, and having acquired smart new premises he was clearing his yard at Finchley. He offered Bert Blower all the remaining Palladium spares, which included several nearly complete cars and commercials, plus tons of engines, axles, gearboxes, radiators and car bodies for £200. After much haggling, Bert bought them for £100 and remembers that it took him all week to load and move them by lorry to his yard at Wood Green. From there he managed to sell a few bits to the small number of local Palladium lorry operators but does not remember seeing a Palladium car by this late stage in the thirties. He finally scrapped the lot for the war effort - so the curtain was finally run down on the London Palladium.

One of the last sizeable line-ups of YEEs in the test shop. Note the pre-Great War Palladium van in the background which was probably kept as the works hack or else had just been taken in part exchange.

Forgotten Names

McNAMARAS

**After 110 years in road transport, the famous London firm of
McNamaras lost its identity in post-war nationalisation.
Before that this 'Haulier of Repute' had one of the largest fleets
on contract hire work, and here CHRIS SALAMAN looks back
over the highlights of its history and at some of
the fascinating vehicles that it ran.**

THERE are but a handful of firms who can trace their 'beginnings' back to the start of the nineteenth century, particularly in the road transport industry.

One such firm that could was the London based firm of McNamara's. It began at premises in Castle Street, Finsbury, where the brothers A & W McNamara traded as cartage contractors.

1837 was, as everyone knows, the year of accession of Queen Victoria to the throne, followed three years later by the introduction of Rowland Hill's 'Penny Post'. McNamara's were amongst the first with a contract to carry the Royal Mails. Previous to this

date, letters had been delivered on a very much more personal basis and were, as a result, far more expensive. Now, with the introduction of Penny

One of McNamara's earliest intake of motor vehicles, a Belsize made in Manchester around 1909. It is working on one of the first contracts to deliver newspapers by motor van.

Part of the giant fleet of Dennis vans prepares to set out on a night run in 1911.

A 1909 line-up in McNamara's yard, showing seven Dennis, a deep radiatored Leyland and, at the extreme ends, two unidentified veterans [the one on the right appears to be a steamer of Serpollet, Cremorne or Clarkson type].

Post, anyone could write to a distant relative or friend by placing their correspondence in an envelope, sticking a penny stamp on it, and posting it in one of the new type letter boxes. It was, in fact, a tremendous leap forward in communications. The work was scrupulously scheduled by the Postmaster General, to whom all contractors were responsible. It was interesting to note that, although this period coincided with the sudden and very rapid growth of the railway system, a large percentage of mail still travelled long distances by road (and did so well into the twentieth century). One of the main reasons for this policy was the fact that many destinations were linked by several different railway companies, which resulted in frequent trans-shipments, a cause of delay to the Mail. Hence the direct and somewhat slower speed of the mail horse coach was invariably preferred. The Brighton mail coach ran up to June 1905 (it took 5½ hours!), when it was superseded by motor van, the carriage of passengers having long since finished. By 1900, McNamara's had some 1300 horses utilised on their mail van services, the majority working in the Greater London area. They started with their first motor van in 1904 and by 1907 there were sixteen motor vans on Post Office work. They were mainly of Leyland and Dennis manufacture and these had increased to sixty-seven in number by 1913, when there were 436 horse-drawn vans. Amongst these, the large pair horse vans introduced in

A portion of the horse-drawn fleet engaged on the mail contract. Horses played an important part in McNamara's affairs into the thirties [there were 240 on the payroll in 1931].

The cheap and tough Morris-Commercial gradually ousted the Dennis from McNamara's C and D fleet in the late twenties. This is a 30 cwt R type.

89

A 1925 Scammell, originally on solids, working on the Birmingham trunk run and carrying some of Sydney Flavel's gas cookers. Note the commercial AA badge.

McNamara's built their own bodies in their Paradise Street depôt and, as this Manchester shows, also carried out maintenance work.

In the early thirties the fleet was extremely varied. Morris-Commercials [like these Royal Mail vans] predominated but there were also Ford As [centre] and Vulcans [left].

An idea of the importance of the mail contract to McNamara's is given by the line-up of Morris-Commercial R types in 1931, when two thirds of their vehicles were engaged on this work.

1887 were by far the most common. They were used predominantly on parcel work between the main sorting offices and main line railway stations.

Whilst the first long distance motor mail vans had started their nightly runs from 1908 onwards, so, too, had the general haulage side of McNamara's with regular nightly services to the south coast towns of Worthing and Brighton. Fresh vegetables for Covent Garden were carried on the return run.

By 1909 McNamara's had virtually standardised on Dennis 30 cwt vehicles, though a few heavier Leylands and Fodens were used, as was a fleet of 6 cwt capacity Auto-Carrier (AC) tricars and 15 cwt capacity Belsize. They were prepared to loan motor vans to potential hirers to convince them of the benefits to be derived. Over £20,000 profit was earned in this way in 1909 and much of this was ploughed back into motor vans, the Dennis fleet having reached 120 by the summer of 1912. A commentator at the time said that these were one of London's most familiar sights, and were even to be seen as far afield as Bristol, whence McNamara's were doing the longest mail motor service from London.

McNamara's still bought Dennis in the late twenties but they tended to be the heavier models. The three tonners have been converted to artics and the one in the middle is a 1927 five tonner. This photo was taken at the Leicester depôt.

A 46 cu ft van on a 20 bhp Singer Junior of 1933 bought by McNamara's for around £120.

Unic had a limited following amongst heavy vehicle operators in London largely on the strength of the success of their taxis. This may be a prison van or bullion carrier.

reporting that between 1908 and 1910 the monthly average of vehicle availability had averaged 98.3 per cent and never dropped below 97.7. All continued to go well until 1913, when the fixed price contract with the GPO began to cause problems and resulted in a loss of £25,000 compared with a profit of £31,000 in the year up to June 1912 and the appointment of a Receiver. The cause had been the rise in the price of fuel and the GPO's habit of calling on vehicles and then only using them sporadically. McNamara's only got paid for the actual mileage they covered and found that, on some services, their vehicles were only actually earning revenue during eight minutes per working hour, for which they received, on average, the princely sum of 4½d! Unfortunately, the contract was fixed until 1917 and by then the Great War made a satisfactory re-quote impossible. However, McNamara's struggled on through shortages of drivers, vehicles, horses and horsemen and were finally reconstituted in 1921 with a considerably reduced fleet.

Up to 1919 much of the general haulage work had been of a localised nature, but on the cessation of hostilities long distance night trunk services soon developed between London, Birmingham, Bristol, Liverpool, Leicester and Bradford, where provincial depôts were duly set up, and these handled 500 tons nightly within a few years.

The horse still had a very important part to play in McNamara's local goods distribution, and it was interesting to note that they thought very highly of their horse-drawn fleet, providing special first floor stables at Castle Street, an unique idea in itself. They also provided a horse hospital and blacksmith's at their Middleton Road stables in Dalston. Every horse owned by McNamara's was identified by a number branded on its hoof and appropriate records were kept for each animal. Drivers took great pride in keeping their horses well groomed (a special vacuum brush was adopted) and harness highly polished, something that won them awards at annual horse van parades. They were still using horses in the thirties and reporting that improved shoes meant that each now only required 3 shoes

A large number of Morris-Commercials converted to three ton artics were run, especially in London. Nodte the curious selection of wheels. The basis appears to be a shortened R type 30 cwt, though it may be a 2 ton TX.

McNamara's bought dozens of Commers in the early thirties [1932 *left*, 1934 *right*], several of which featured Duralumin bodies following the success of an experimental model in 1932.

A Leyland Beaver of 1933 in the long distance truck fleet. It is hard to decide if it is a low van or high side truck, though the former is presumably more likely if the load is really perishable Shredded Wheat.

per month compared with the 6½ previously.

By the twenties McNamara's had diversified into three main types of operation. Firstly, there was the Inner London Mail Contract, employing approximately 300 vehicles, both horse and motor, on varying mail carrying duties.

Secondly, there was a very large contract hire section which hired vans and lorries to many large businesses who only provided their own drivers, thus avoiding the aggravation of maintenance problems when running their own vehicle. The vehicles ranged in size from three wheeled vans to 'Black Marias' for the police and prison services! McNamara's was also the first motor van contractor to hire to the national newspapers, having carried *The Globe* in Edwardian days.

Lastly, there was the general haulage and parcel service that connected London to most of the large

No urban collection and delivery fleet was complete without the familiar Scammell mechanical horse. This is a three tonner of 1934.

Like many vehicles in the fleet, this Scammell has had its identity hidden by a McNamara radiator badge. It is one of the old chain drive petrol engined tractors converted to Mercedes-Benz diesel power.

provincial centres. This service also included specialised warehousing and Customs and shipping services. Goods were collected in small C&D (Collection and Delivery) vehicles, mostly of Morris-Commercial manufacture, the one ton chassis being popular (presumably through the use of identical models on Post Office work) and brought back to the loading banks at the varying depôts where parcels were sorted for trans-shipment onto the overnight trunk vehicles, usually Scammells.

In 1930 McNamara's was once again restructured with a reduction in capital because they were concerned about growing long distance competition, particularly from the railways, whose lobbying of the government was paying dividends. McNamara's now had 520,000 10/- shares, of which 250,000 were allocated. The 1931 fleet consisted of 240 horses and 450 motor vehicles, and of these 300 were employed on GPO work. The lorries and vans comprised Dennis, Morris-Commercial, Leyland, Manchester, the new Commer Raider, Ford, Austin, Scammell, Vulcan, Mercedes-Benz and Sentinel. The Mercedes had been bought to gain diesel experience and on the strength of this one of the Scammells had its petrol unit swapped for a Mercedes diesel in McNamara's extensive workshops. How successful this proved to be is long since forgotten, but in general the vehicles were very reliable with, for example, only four breakdowns out of 12,000 mail services in Christmas week 1930.

The firm enjoyed very good staff and customer relations and was very keen to promote road safety. Each of the 500-600 drivers carried the insurance papers for his vehicle in a sealed tube in the cab and if the seal ever had to be broken for any reason he had to make a full report to the transport manager. Drivers had to pass McNamara's own test long before the Ministry of Transport had conceived theirs. In 1930, company drivers were involved in four fatal accidents and seventeen claims for personal injury, but out of 6 million miles covered in 1934 there were only two fatalities and 10 claims. Staff had

There was a brief craze for motorcycle-based parcel cars and these are believed to be 10 cwt Fleets made by Ariel in 1934 using their 557cc single cylinder engine. A very similar machine was also made by Croft. Before the Great War, McNamara's had run the broadly similar Auto Carriers.

As well as the lighter Raiders and Centaurs, McNamara's ran some bigger Commers. This four tonner was new in 1935 and photographed for their Jubilee celebrations in 1937.

A view of the Bristol depôt with trilby hatted foreman and Vulcans and Scammells in evidence. Note the advanced thinking that had gone into efficient undercover freight handling. On the subject of Bristol, our thanks to the Bristol Vintage Bus Group for preserving many of the photos used in this feature.

McNamara's bought several Mercedes-Benz Miracle five ton capacity diesel artics in 1933 no doubt to replace their ageing Morris conversions.

In the workshops at King John's Court. Monobloc engines were reconditioned *in situ* with the aid of a Black and Decker cylinder honer. The 1934 Bedford was, surprisingly, one of very few of this make in the fleet. Note the ominous 'Liverpool Virus' Morris-Commercial peddling nothing more sinister than 2/6d tins of rat poison and 1/6d tins of mice poison.

A smart 25 cwt Commer looking somehow more modern than its 1935 registration might suggest. No doubt it survived into the era of McNamara's nationalisation.

been given paid holidays since 1919, long before this was mandatory, and there was a pleasant 'family atmosphere' in the firm with lots of communal activities. One of the most popular of these was the McNamara Entertainers who gave concert parties and popular plays like *Lord Richard in the Pantry* for charity.

By 1936 there were one or two clouds on the horizon for McNamara's. To win the mail contract, certain parts of which lasted until 1943, they had to submit a considerably reduced quote. The new licensing laws meant that they were continually in traffic courts answering their objectors, usually the railway

companies, and having to prove that a need existed for the licences they required to carry on.

However, the firm and its 1200 employees celebrated its centenary in 1937 with a grand gala dinner at which the only sour note was struck by a speech from Ernest Bevin, then General Secretary of the Transport Workers Union, who said that if he had his way he 'would nationalise all the transport system' and that he understood that 'the most efficient service was the Post Office', though he omitted to mention that much of this efficiency was due to free enterprise from McNamara's. In 1948 his wish was granted and much of McNamara's was merged with Carter Paterson to become BRS Parcels Ltd, whilst the trunk vehicles all went to BRS General Haulage's Hampstead, Kentish Town and Tufnell Park branches.

INDEX

Index to
VINTAGE LORRY ANNUAL 1

First edition copyright Marshall Harris & Baldwin Ltd 1980
ISBN 0 906116 21 X

Published by: Marshall Harris & Baldwin Ltd.
17 Air Street
London, W.1.
Registered in London 1410311
Designed by Brian Harris and Mark Slade
Printed by: Plaistow Press Ltd., New Plaistow Road, London, E.15.